CW01239142

THE STORY OF *The* AMERICA'S CUP

THE STORY OF *The* AMERICA'S CUP
1851–2007

PAINTINGS BY Tim Thompson
WRITTEN BY Ranulf Rayner
FOREWORD BY Ted Turner

David Bateman

To my lovely and long suffering wife, Annette,
who kindly sketched the portraits for this book.

Published in 2007 by David Bateman Ltd,
30 Tarndale Grove, Albany, Auckland, New Zealand.

© Ranulf Rayner 1986, 1991, 1995, 2000, 2003, 2007
© David Bateman Ltd 2007

This book is copyright. Except for the purpose of fair review, no part may be stored or transmitted in any form or by any means, electronic or mechanical, including recording or storage in any information retrieval systems, without permission in writing from the publisher. No reproduction may be made, whether by photocopying or by any other means, unless a licence has been obtained from the publisher or its agent.

ISBN 978-1-86953-670-1

Line illustrations by Ethan Danielson, Ranulf Rayner and
 Annette Rayner
Book designed by Michael Head
Printed in China through Everbest Printing Co.

CONTENTS

Foreword by Ted Turner	7
Introduction	8
The Artist	9
The Research	10
Rogues' Gallery	13
The 'Ladies'	22
The Courses	25
The International America's Cup Class	31
The Paintings	33
1851 *America* defeats the British Fleet in a single race	34
1870 *Magic* defeats *Cambria* (Great Britain) 1-0	36
1871 *Columbia* and *Sappho* defeat *Livonia* (Great Britain) 4-1	38
1876 *Madeleine* defeats *Countess of Dufferin* (Canada) 2-0	40
1881 *Mischief* defeats *Atalanta* (Canada) 2-0	42
1885 *Puritan* defeats *Genesta* (Great Britain) 2-0	44
1886 *Mayflower* defeats *Galatea* (Great Britain) 2-0	46
1887 *Volunteer* defeats *Thistle* (Great Britain) 2-0	48
1893 *Vigilant* defeats *Valkyrie II* (Great Britain) 3-0	50
1895 *Defender* defeats *Valkyrie III* (Great Britain) 3-0	52
1899 *Columbia* defeats *Shamrock* (Northern Ireland) 3-0	54
1901 *Columbia* defeats *Shamrock II* (Northern Ireland) 3-0	56
1903 *Reliance* defeats *Shamrock III* (Northern Ireland) 3-0	58
1920 *Resolute* defeats *Shamrock IV* (Northern Ireland) 3-2	60
1930 *Enterprise* defeats *Shamrock V* (Northern Ireland) 4-0	62
1934 *Rainbow* defeats *Endeavour* (Great Britain) 4-2	64
1937 *Ranger* defeats *Endeavour II* (Great Britain) 4-0	66
1958 *Columbia* defeats *Sceptre* (Great Britain) 4-0	68
1962 *Weatherly* defeats *Gretel* (Australia) 4-1	70
1964 *Constellation* defeats *Sovereign* (Great Britain) 4-0	72
1967 *Intrepid* defeats *Dame Pattie* (Australia) 4-0	74
1970 *Intrepid* defeats *Gretel II* (Australia) 4-1	76
1974 *Courageous* defeats *Southern Cross* (Australia) 4-0	78
1977 *Courageous* defeats *Australia* (Australia) 4-0	80
1980 *Freedom* defeats *Australia* (Australia) 4-0	82
1983 *Australia II* (Australia) defeats *Liberty* 4-3	84
1987 *Stars & Stripes* defeats *Kookaburra III* (Australia) 4-0	86
1988 *Stars & Stripes* defeats *New Zealand* (New Zealand) 3-0	88
1992 *America³* defeats *Il Moro di Venezia* (Italy) 4-1	90
1995 *Black Magic* (New Zealand) defeats *Young America* 5-0	92
2000 *Black Magic* (New Zealand) defeats *Luna Rossa* (Italy) 5-0	94
2003 *Alinghi* (Switzerland) defeats *NZL 82* (New Zealand) 5-0	96
2007 *Alinghi* (Switzerland) defeats *NZL 92* (New Zealand) 5-2	98

FOREWORD

Historically the America's Cup has been a battlefield of wits, muscle and money. But on the other side of the coin is a face of exceptional character and beauty. I can think of no finer artist to portray this side than Tim Thompson and his magnificent paintings of dramatic moments from each challenge since 1851 are absolutely unparalleled.

As a yachtsman and adventurer, The America's Cup has dominated many years of my life and, right from the time I first dipped my toe in the cold waters off Newport with *Mariner* in 1974, I was hooked on it. I suppose therefore that winning with *Courageous* in 1977 was the realisation of a dream, and the closest that I shall ever get to heaven.

I bought *Courageous* after that event not through sentiment, but because at the time I was convinced we could repeat the victory. However, those old ladies the 12 Meters are always up to new tricks and, over-taken in 1980 by the sheer acceleration of modern technology, it turned out that I was wrong.

The America's Cup has no second prize, and the designers and their sponsors will no doubt continue to try and bash each other's brains out with increasing ferocity. Sure we would all be much happier without the space age, but life is not like that, and those that cannot escape from it can only strive to do the job better than the next man.

Fortunately I can escape, for on the walls of my office I have other beautiful paintings by Tim Thompson. To me his work is an endless source of pleasure, as I am sure it will be for those lucky enough to acquire this book.

Ted Turner

INTRODUCTION

As idle as a painted ship
Upon a painted ocean

Inspiration usually comes to me in my bath. The evening that I lay there pondering on the above words from 'The Rime of the Ancient Mariner', by Samuel Taylor Coleridge, was no exception.

Painted ships had no right to be idle, I thought, and painted yachts should fly. The Ancient Mariner was wrong; a painting was no more exciting to him than a dead albatross. Perhaps, if we could paint famous racing yachts, and capture on canvas epic moments from the history of the greatest yacht race in the world, the America's Cup, 'We'd *be* the first, that ever burst *out* of that silent sea'.

By the time I stopped dreaming and stepped ashore, my bath was as cold as an iceberg.

My first reaction, before turning in, was to telephone Tim Thompson. He always worked late, very often until the birds started singing in the morning. 'I have an idea", I said.

My interest in marine painting began when my father died. With my wife and two sons I had moved to our family house in Devonshire, built by my parents the year I was born. Sadly, many of the paintings I had grown up with had gone elsewhere, and the bare walls filled us with gloom.

When we moved to Ashcombe one of the first alterations we made was to convert an old squash court into a studio with a panoramic window facing the sea. The house stands at almost a thousand feet above sea level and being only three miles from the coast has breath-taking views. Inspired by this setting, I thought of painting some canvases myself, for I had won a landscape prize at school but I was too busy farming, and out of practice, so I felt that the results would be similarly 'muddy'!

Fortunately we had been left one beautiful painting, by Peter Monamy, of warships in Torbay. It hung over the fireplace in our dining room, and it cried out for some nautical companions. Then we heard of Thompson, a young marine artist who lived in Cornwall. He sounded promising, for apparently he painted in the manner of the old masters, but sadly we had no idea how to find him.

One winter's day, we sat down with our telephone books and called almost every Thompson in Cornwall. 'Are you Thompson the artist?' I would enquire. 'No, are you Bones the Butcher?' some joker would reply. But at last we found him under the initial 'T', and we arranged to meet him at his cottage high up on the edge of Dartmoor.

THE ARTIST

Tim Thompson impressed us. His warm handshake and open friendly face made us feel immediately at home, and his enthusiasm for our proposal was infectious. Although he had none of his work to show us, and seldom has even today, he left us in no doubt that he could achieve exceptional results.

Tim, who was born in Hull in 1951, told me that for many years he had lived on the tiny island of Herm in the Channel Islands, where, as a boy, he had become fascinated by the moods of the sea, and had taught himself to paint. In Guernsey he had trained for a diploma in horticulture, and in 1975 had moved with his wife Sharon to take up a job in Devonshire with the Plymouth Parks Department. An accident had now forced him to retire, and as a result he had decided to turn his painting hobby into a full-time career.

The two coastal scenes he painted for us were an astonishing success. So great was the admiration for them that we decided to cover all our bare walls with 'Thompsons', but not at our own expense! We would obtain other commissions for Tim, and in return he would give us some paintings, which I and my wife, herself an accomplished artist, would specify. It was a splendidly old-fashioned way of starting a collection, and it worked so well that we decided to stage an exhibition for Tim, to be held during July 1983 at Cowes on the Isle of Wight.

Once, with my two brothers, I had been the proud owner of an 8 metre yacht, but after an unhappy adventure one cold night in January, involving two lifeboats, a Brixham trawler and a number of good ladies with blankets, my family had since been reduced to a vulgar bright-red speedboat, which we had bought in order to advertise our strawberry farm along the crowded South Devon beaches. We now used the *Strawberry*, as she was somewhat obviously called, to ship the entire exhibition to Cowes. As we crossed the choppy waters of the Solent, those driving their smart Admiral's Cup yachts determinedly across our bows must have thought our little craft, weighed down with paintings, rather an unusual sight!

A good friend of mine, Robin Rising, the efficient Secretary of the Royal Yacht Squadron, had kindly arranged for us to hold our exhibition in the heart of the yachting world at the Cowes Week Regatta offices. But we had to be out before Cowes Week itself, when the racing started and the competitors arrived. It gave us little time for selling, but as I had by now persuaded Tim to change from painting mostly eighteenth-century warships to concentrate more on yachts, the opportunity to show off his work to professional yachtsmen made the exhibition seem very worthwhile.

At first we attracted little interest, but soon Tim was accepting compliments and the paintings began to sell. Then on the fifth and final day of the exhibition Ted Turner walked in.

'Say, I'll have that one in the window', said the lean-looking American. 'Sorry,' replied Sharon, Tim's wife, 'it's already sold.' 'Then let's have that one on the wall', he said. 'Pity,' replied Sharon, 'that's also sold.' 'Hell,' exclaimed the stranger loudly, 'what is this — a charity?' Several interested people who were looking at the paintings now turned their heads, and suddenly there was a hush and you could hear a pin drop. 'I'll tell you what's wrong around here, you're not charging enough,' he cracked. 'By the time I return back down the street, I want to see your prices doubled!'

He came back half an hour later, but there was not a painting left! Our splendid American friend was not to be deterred. 'Those paintings were fantastic,' he said, and as he left through the door he asked Tim for a painting of 'the Battle of the Nile' and also to paint him a 'large one' of Trafalgar. 'Who on earth was that?' I questioned a lady, who was following him. 'You don't know who that was?' she exclaimed. 'That was the owner of the Atlanta Braves baseball team, winner of the America's Cup in '77, none other than the great Ted Turner.'

Ted has since asked us to send him ten more paintings, and it was his request, soon after we had returned from Cowes, where the America's Cup had first been conceived, that Tim should paint *Courageous*, the Cup winner in both 1974 and 1977, that gave me the idea, in my bath, for this book.

Tim has held other exhibitions, and his paintings are already selling all over the world, but in no way has this affected him. On the contrary, he remains one of the nicest and most modest men I have ever met, and his capacity for work is astonishing. His ultimate ambition is to paint as well as, if not better than, any marine artist alive, but meanwhile he intends to reduce his output and take an annual holiday with his wife and two daughters.

Tim, who now lives in a nice house overlooking the Tamar river, was thrilled with the idea that he should paint epic moments from the history of the America's Cup, although it meant that the paintings would not be sold for a long time, at least until after the book was written. It also meant that together we would have to carry out a daunting amount of research over a long period.

THE RESEARCH

There is no shortage of information available about the America's Cup, but very little of it seems to be in any one place. My first job, therefore, particularly as I was going to have to specify a large number of paintings, was to log all the books, articles, press cuttings, photographs, pictures, prints, models, plans, drawings, films, videos, letters and personal accounts about the race that could be tracked down.

The gargantuan task took far longer than anticipated, and just as I had the index neatly arranged on my new computer, my son's Burmese cat decided to go for a stroll on the keyboard, and in an instant my weeks of research had vanished from the screen. It is fortunate that man learned to fend for himself before the days of such belligerent machines, and as a result I was able to drown my sorrows with a very stiff drink. But what was more it urged me to get off my cavalry behind and, having soundly reprimanded the cat, I set off for Cowes to look up Robin Rising again.

The library of the Royal Yacht Squadron is a very memorable and historic place. If you can somehow avoid sinking too deeply into the leather armchairs and dozing off, it is possible to see so much happening on the Medina river and out over the Solent, that reading becomes difficult. Probably just as well, for I found books that had not been opened for ages, not covered in dust, the Squadron is far too ship-shape for that, but lurking in dark corners and stuffed with old letters, one of which dated back a hundred years.

It was this letter, written in great detail and high dudgeon, that made me avert my eyes from the superb pictures hanging on the walls and the magic water beyond. If the America's Cup was brimming with such bloody-mindedness, why should we not attempt to show it? How appropriate it would be to the spirit of the contest if Tim's paintings captured battling racing yachts at the most significant moment of truth or protest, of triumph or disaster.

Tim is himself a bit of a historian, and we both began collecting material is if there was no tomorrow. Already he had shelves of well-illustrated books on seafaring, and to these we added every manual, chronicle, chart or ship's drawing that we could lay our hands on. Together we also took hundreds of detailed photographs, and we surprised the owner of one lovely yacht when he found us poised with a camera and for no apparent reason trying to get a close-up shot of his deck.

Another of our joint expeditions was to see the young American, Elizabeth Meyer, and her amazing project to rebuild *Endeavour*. She had written of the J-Class in *Nautical Quarterly*, a leading American magazine: 'These extraordinary yachts, so few in number, were built, with one exception, to contend for the America's Cup. In muscle, beauty and speed, the 'J's' exceeded all the superlatives – they were like skyscrapers, rainbows, bridges, St Paul's Cathedral. They were powerful in every way.' As she admitted, she was swept off her feet the moment she first saw *Endeavour*, while writing that story.

After years of decay, but having already been rescued from the mud, *Endeavour* had looked a forlorn sight, but Elizabeth Meyer, not short of money, was one day determined to see her 'racing up Buzzard's Bay again on the afternoon sou'wester'. Under a tarpaulin and overlooking the Solent from her concrete pad, *Endeavour* was stripped of all but the smallest fragment of her original hull, and then rib by rib, plate by plate, meticulously put together again. Tim and myself, accompanied by eighty-year-old Frank Murdoch, Sir Tom Sopwith's past—and Elizabeth Meyer's present—technical advisor, watched in awe as her exquisite lines began to take shape, and our thoughts drifted back to those sacred days, when gentlemen had fun.

Endeavour has not only been the only 'J' destined to return from oblivion. On another occasion we watched *Velsheda*, against whom she had once raced, having her immense mast stepped for the first time since the 1930s, and later I was able to take some useful photographs of her as I sailed a boat close under her counter. Elizabeth Meyer was right; if she had her way it would not be long, after an interval of more than fifty years, before these amazing yachts were at one another's throats again.

Wherever I travelled I found new gems of information, always helped by nice people, some of whom had fought for the America's Cup and two of whom had won. Graham Mann, who had skippered *Sceptre* in 1958, and whose competent daughter, Sarah, worked for my new yachting business, Mayfair Marine, in London, allowed me to spend hours exploring his library, as did June Goodson, widow of *Sceptre*'s originator, and Bob Ward, secretary of the Royal Thames, the first club ever to have challenged for the Cup. Bob Fisher, yachting correspondent and man of many parts, also allowed me free access to his files, and Ian Dear, author of *Enterprise to Endeavour* and *An Informal History of the America's Cup*, kindly gave me his permission to use the odd anecdote from his own vivid narrative. Everywhere I was generously lent precious manuscripts, but no one could have helped more than Frank Murdoch and Patrick Egan, who had both crewed on the mighty 'J's' in their heyday, and whose detailed records and unbounded enthusiasm had finally encouraged me to 'illustrate' Tim's paintings with this book.

Three of Frank Murdoch's unique photographs were particularly valuable for, taken in 1934, by a spectator through a telescope, they described better than any words the fateful luffing incident that could, and many say should, have won Tom Sopwith the America's Cup. It was from these somewhat foreshortened pictures that Tim was able to paint the event, reproduced later, under Murdoch's watchful eye.

I felt that no research would be complete without a visit to the battlefields that for 132 years were the home of the America's Cup. And although the United States were not strange to me, I sensed, somehow, that my mission to New York and Rhode Island would not be without excitement. Arriving at Kennedy Airport around midnight in a snowstorm, I leapt, without thinking, into the first vehicle purporting to be a taxi. It wasn't, and somewhere in Manhattan, beneath the forbidding shapes of the towering skyscrapers, I was dumped without my wallet, and also minus the folder containing the only copy of the initial chapters of my book! But although I knew about such dangers, the city seemed cleaner and more vibrant than before, and my reception at the New York Yacht Club, much as it must have been for those who had tried and failed to remove the Cup, was only one of mild surprise and greatest sympathy.

Frank Murdoch had kindly arranged for me to be the guest of Commodore Henry H. Anderson Jr and no one could have been more charming or a better host. Also Chairman of the American Sail Training Association, and Vice-President of the International Yacht Racing Union (IYRU), he had served on the America's Cup committee for several years and was long-standing President of the World 12 Metre Association. He asked me to look him up later in Newport, and it was there, in the nostalgic atmosphere of the Reading Room, that because of his assiduous help and many introductions, I was able to pick up the threads again from my interrupted story.

Among the many who assisted me on Rhode Island were Halsey Herreshoff, grandson of the famous builder of so many America's Cup defenders and a crew member on several winners since, and Tom Benson, a director of the newly established Museum of Yachting in Jamestown. Newport itself breathes of the Cup, and wherever you go there are reminders of the special role this beautiful little town, with its white clapboard houses, its wharfs and lobster bars, has more recently played and will continue to play, even if the event, with its massive input of cash to the local economy, has temporarily departed. A great seaport before the American Revolution, for a time it was inhabited by the Navy, but gone now are the sleazy dens and the tattoo parlours, and it remains just a sleepy fishing port, living perhaps a little on its past, when the super-rich built their 'summer cottages' nearby overlooking the ocean. Before leaving I went to see Marble House, the Vanderbilt cottage, finished in 1892 for the staggering amount, even by today's standards, of eleven million dollars. As one of the smaller William K. Vanderbilt houses, which ranged from Fifth Avenue to Florida, it made me aware of the fabulous wealth that lay behind many of the America's Cup defences, and as Harold S. Vanderbilt stared down from the wall close to the polished wheel off *Ranger*, I felt, as many challengers must have felt, remarkably humble.

From Newport I drove back south again along the wooded New England coastline to Mystic, where again all those I had arranged to see could not have been more helpful. Mystic has an excellent maritime museum, a nautical shop and picture gallery, but more importantly one of the leading marine reference libraries in the world, where I was able to unearth more race details and examine some original ship's plans. Many of these I took with me and when a few days later, I returned to the New York Yacht Club, I felt that no stone had been left unturned. But as Mr Hohri, the Club's brilliant librarian was to point out, that could not have been further from the truth.

The New York Club, fronting onto West Forty-Fourth Street in mid-town Manhattan, has a grand air about it, that invites hushed whispers and a reverence that any challenger must have found hard to take. From an impressive entrance hall there leads off a passage to the members' dining room, built with heavy beams like the gun deck of a man-o-war, and up one flight of curving stairs is the lofty echoing model room, resplendent with its carvings and massive marble fireplace and where only the brave dare tread. Here live the accurate scale models of all the famous boats that have fought for the America's Cup, each with its respective adversary lying passively alongside in a glass case. I was quickly 'arrested' for sketching the models (no cameras are allowed), and when I explained to the custodian that I was the guest of the Commodore, his suspicions only became greater. 'You know, I'm not Alan Bond', I said. Of course the Aussies have left their mark in the Club, and nearby in a cabinet, close to the small hexagonal room reserved for the America's Cup, there sits a symbolic 'effigy', a silver winged keel kindly presented by the premier of Western Australia.

Apart from sketching the models, however, I hoped to be allowed to spend some time in the Club's historic library. Situated on an upper deck, it was mercifully the most traditional and friendly room that I entered during my entire visit to the United States. Mr Hohri piled up mountains of scrap books for me to pore over, each cross-referenced in the most efficient way, and sitting beside a fine model of the *Virginia*, a steam yacht once owned by my family, I took endless notes from press cuttings dating well back into the last century. One photograph I came cross must have been that from which the race committee made their decision to disqualify *Gretel II* after she had won a race in 1970, and it was later used by Tim Thompson in order to effect his authoritative painting of that controversial event.

I returned home on Thanksgiving Day, after sharing roast turkey and pumpkin pie with some delightful American friends. I trusted that perhaps, if the airport security officials were feeling generous, when I arrived back at Kennedy and handed in my sketches of that fake taxi I had taken and its 'Gypsy' driver, at least they might be able to retrieve the first chapters of my book – but no such luck. They caught him later, but like other 'pirates' shortly to be described here, having read all about it he probably now squandering the cash on a boat for the America's Cup!

ROGUES' GALLERY

The colourful characters that have taken part in the America's Cup throughout its long history are too numerous to mention in any detail, but surely it must be worth including some of them in our rogues' gallery. At least the reader may then understand, before delving deeper into the story of each match, the stuff of which these men were made.

Starting with the first match, some were good men, some not so good, but all are noted for one splendid quality, the desire to win at all costs.

John C. Stevens

John Stevens was one of four brothers, the sons of Colonel John Stevens, a famous inventor who had been a leading figure in the Republic's early history and who had built their family home at Castle Point, New Jersey, near where the Stevens Institute of Technology is still situated. John Stevens Jr had become interested in sailing when still a young man and had first owned a twenty-footer called the *Diver*, later building larger boats, some with his own hands, until he had become somewhat of a yachting authority and had graduated to a splendid schooner, the *Gimcrack*. It was on this yacht on 30 July 1844 that Stevens with eight friends formed the New York Yacht Club and was appointed its first Commodore.

New York was already becoming the financial hub of America, and by 1850 Commodore Stevens had made a considerable fortune from shipbuilding, treating himself to a town house which was little short of a palace. But although so well-heeled, he considered it prudent to form a syndicate with five of his friends, when, because of his desire to show off American vessels, he decided to build the yacht *America* to race against the British in 1851, the year of the Great Exhibition.

Stevens was an ardent gambler and after his arrival in England it must have been a great disappointment to him when, as George Schuyler, a member of his syndicate, said 'with his usual promptness, and regardless of the pockets of his associates', he posted a wager in the Royal Yacht Squadron and there were no takers. But he collected the One Hundred Guinea Cup, and at least must have attributed some value to it – for in 1857 it was Commodore John Stevens with his syndicate who presented the bottomless jug, now known as the America's Cup, to the New York Yacht Club for international competition in yacht racing.

George L. Schuyler

After the gallant Commodore Stevens died at the age of seventy-two in 1857, George Schuyler, who had first arranged the deal with William Brown, *America*'s builder, volunteered to be a trustee of the document which the syndicate had signed on the Cup's presentation, now known as the first Deed of Gift. At thirty-nine Schuyler had been the youngest member of the syndicate, and he was in an excellent position to ensure fair play in the future.

Grandson of a general who had made his name in the Revolutionary Wars, George Schuyler had used his considerable inheritance to develop a number of steamship companies and as a result he was an astute negotiator. It was just as well, for right from the start the Cup matches were plagued with endless disputes, largely caused by the possessiveness of the New York Yacht Club and the piratical tendencies of many of the challengers.

George Schuyler's contribution is remembered through the Fort Schuyler Foundation, and his name was painted on the transom of Liberty in the 1983 match as a memorial to the man who prevented the event from becoming a rough-house and thus saved the Cup for posterity. When he died at sea in 1890, having witnessed seven successful defences, he had done more for making the races a test of international skill in design and helmsmanship than anyone in the Cup's history.

Lieutenant William Henn
William Henn appears in this gallery only because his challenge was perhaps the most unusual.

Born in Ireland, Henn had served in the Royal Navy from the age of thirteen and had spent many years south of the Equator, being second-in-command of the expedition sent to find Doctor David Livingstone in 1872. On retiring three years later, and still enamoured by the sea, he was determined to cruise the oceans permanently, and for seven years he lived on board a small yawl, with his wife and her pets, travelling some 50,000 miles.

Henn had probably been put up to challenging for the Cup by the designer of his subsequent and larger yacht *Galatea*, which had expediently been paid for by his wife. He was a leisurely fellow and racing was not his scene, so when he sent off his application through the Royal Northern Yacht Club it must have raised a few eyebrows.

As a challenger for the world's premier yachting trophy, *Galatea* did not exactly put the wind up the opposition, particularly when Henn sailed her across the Atlantic complete with his wife, the first lady to have done so, and their animals, including a monkey, amongst the crew. Many Americans thought that her cheerful owner must be bluffing, but when *Galatea* was towed out for her first race and Henn declared that she had never been faster, it was found out to be true.

14

Lieutenant and Mrs Henn

The Earl of Dunraven
Before he started racing yachts, Wyndham Thomas Wyndham-Quin, fourth Earl of Dunraven, who had succeeded his Catholic father in 1871, had enjoyed an adventurous career. At a tender age he had been removed by his father from his Protestant mother and had been sent to school in Rome, where he developed an aggressive personality and an obstinate disregard for the rules.

It had been intended originally that Dunraven should become a violinist, but on returning to Ireland he forsook the bow for small boats and soon ruined his hands by hauling on the halyards and sweating on the sheets. One of his first boats had a habit of running aground so he always carried 'legs' and christened her the *Cripple*. He enjoyed his 'desperate moments' and at the age of twenty-six he became the *Daily Telegraph* war correspondent, reporting on the British-Abyssinian War, and later on the Franco-Prussian War of 1870.

In 1871, he inherited his father's Irish estate with a valuable stud farm, afterwards becoming an accomplished steeplechaser, and in the same year he took off to America to go big game hunting under the watchful eye of Buffalo Bill Cody, a famous Indian tracker. They shot elk in Nebraska and Dunraven was so captivated with the wide open spaces that he returned later and bought 60,000 acres for a game reserve near Colorado. His passion for the chase, and is interest in game conservation encouraged him to start writing again and this in turn developed into a zeal for public speaking.

It was while he was in politics that he began racing large yachts. He had not been popular with his party, the Liberals, once resigning on a matter of principle when Under-Secretary for the Colonies. He set about his new-found sport with unusual spirit and on arrival in New York with *Valkyrie II* in 1893 he quickly made his presence known. It was not long before the race committee were saying harsh things about him. As his crew were behaving similarly, he had them given a daily 'Valkyrie cocktail', described briefly by Dunraven in his extensive memoirs as a 'nauseous black-dose, concocted in a tin'. Such 'medicine' did not endear him to either the British or American public, however, as can be discovered from the stories of 1893 and 1895 told later in this book.

Dunraven

Nathanael Greene Herreshoff

At the same time that the noble Earl was building *Valkyrie II*, a new yacht designer was entering the field in America. The two Herreshoff brothers, taking advantage of their education at the Massachusetts Institute of Technology, had started off their careers constructing steam vessels, but in 1891 Nathanael produced a yacht called the *Gloriana* which won all her races by miles. His reputation spread rapidly, and as a result, when Dunraven's challenge was received at the close of 1892, two syndicates chose Nat Herreshoff to design them prospective defenders; one, the Vanderbilt yacht, being named *Colonia*, and the other, commissioned by a syndicate headed by C. Oliver Iselin, being named *Vigilant*.

Vigilant was the first yacht to be constructed entirely of bronze, and her subsequent victory in the America's Cup immediately put Herreshoff's name in the history books. But 'the Bronze Beauty' was only the beginning. By 1903 Herreshoff, working from his Rhode Island yard, had already designed and built three Cup winners, and had come to be hailed as 'the Wizard of Bristol'. It was the year in which he launched the mighty *Reliance*, probably the most impressive America's Cup yacht that will ever be seen, and it was generally acknowledged by then that there was no one else in the United States with such fertile imagination and with such a clever disregard for accepted principles.

Nat always worked from home and first made a pencil sketch of every yacht he built. This was then turned into a wooden model before being sent down to the yard, where 200 men were employed. When he died at the age of ninety, leaving some 18,000 sketches, Nat Herreshoff had designed six successful defenders and by 1934 his yard, the Herreshoff Manufacturing Company, had built no fewer than eight Cup winners – a colossal achievement in any terms.

Sir Thomas Lipton

While Herreshoff was doing his damnedest to prevent the British taking back the Cup, Sir Thomas Lipton was embarking on the most determined attempt to retrieve it from the Yankees.

Lipton's story reads like a film script. Born in Glasgow in 1850, the son of poor Irish parents, he started his working life as an errand boy but soon got bored and set sail for America as a steerage passenger on a steam packet. There he worked on rice and tobacco plantations before moving to New York to help as a clerk in a grocery store. Four years later he returned to Glasgow, where, then aged nineteen, he opened his own provision shop, quickly discovering that his pleasant smile and ready wit were attracting an unusual number of customers. Promotion was the name of Lipton's game, and before long he was able to open more stores and afford more publicity. It has been said that Lipton was the pioneer of pictorial advertising and the clever posters which he placed in his shop windows did much to lay the foundations of his future tea and grocery empire.

Although he was no yachtsman the America's Cup had always intrigued him, and as his empire grew so did his ambition to build a boat and 'lift the auld mug'. At last in 1899 the opportunity arrived and thus started his determined campaign which was to comprise five challenges, raise the Cup to great esteem and, as he later noted in his autobiography, be his 'principle recreation for over thirty years'.

Lipton was fifty-one at the time of his first challenge and he had already been knighted for his many generous deeds. He was a man of utter integrity and unbounded enthusiasm, and the world, particularly the Americans, who soon regarded him as a legend, came to adore him. Harold S. Vanderbilt, writing in his book *Enterprise* after retaining the Cup in 1930, the year of Lipton's last challenge, stated: 'In spite of all the Cup stands for, the greater part of the American people would have been glad to see it take flight, only because of their love, their sympathy, and their admiration for that grand old sportsman, Sir Thomas Lipton, who had spent so many years and so many millions on such a futile quest.' Lipton returned home to England directly afterwards, with a cup presented to him by the American people for trying, and died a bachelor in October 1931 aged eighty-one, with the plans for *Shamrock VI* already very much on his mind.

Harold S. Vanderbilt

Harold S. Vanderbilt, 'Mike' to his friends, was only fifteen when Sir Thomas Lipton brought his first *Shamrock* over to America, and he grew up very much in awe of the famous grocer. Born in 1884, he was the great-grandson of the 'Commodore', Cornelius Vanderbilt, who had made his vast fortune exploiting the ideas of the Stevens family in railroad and steamship design.

Vanderbilt's father had complained that money left him nothing to live for and that his great wealth had led only to unhappiness, but luckily young Harold inherited the family fortune with none of his father's abject misery attached. On the contrary, Vanderbilt was a man of enormous energy with a highly analytical mind, and having left Harvard with a law degree, he lived life to the full, becoming a director of the New York Central Railroad.

The 1930s were perhaps the water-shed of modern yacht design and Vanderbilt was probably the first man to take the management of a large racing boat into the modern era. He ran his yachts on the lines of a big company and nothing was left off the agenda. Everything had to be immaculate and only the latest type of equipment was fitted – as on *Enterprise*, his first defender, which had an amazing duralumin mast and an even more innovative boom. His crews were also selected with considerable care and each wore a number appropriate to this task, which if not performed entirely to Vanderbilt's satisfaction ended in a rapid trip ashore. Above all, Vanderbilt believed in delegation, and it was largely because of his implicit trust in his afterguard that he was able to concentrate on steering his boats almost to perfection.

Standing stiffly at the helm in his white flannels and blue jacket with commodore's stripes on his sleeve, he would manoeuvre his magnificent yachts with impressive ease, and his starts, as depicted in the painting of the 1937 match, were usually judged with uncanny accuracy. Sir Fisher Dike wrote in his book *Observer on Ranger*: 'Vanderbilt very rarely indeed looks at anything else but his compass, and sails the boat by that, the feel of the helm, and the suggestions of his afterguard. I saw him look at *Endeavour* only a very few times and then just a quick turn of the head was enough. If he wants to know where the enemy is he asks and gets the answer.' There were moments when he made the British look like beginners.

Vanderbilt successfully defended the Cup three times, and amongst his other notable achievements were a revised set of racing rules, still in use today, and the invention of Contract Bridge. 'Gentlemen', he had once said on a steamship cruise to Cuba, 'let me show you a new game.' If the challengers for the America's Cup had overheard, they may have considered that his new game was just another version of 'cat and mouse'!

Sir Thomas Sopwith
While in the process of writing this book I was particularly fortunate to have lunch with Sir T.O.M. Sopwith, then aged ninety-eight. He was in cracking form and full of wonderful anecdotes from the thirties, but he has always shunned publicity, and it occurred to me what a tragedy it would be if any part of his story remained unrecorded. Needless to say the wine was good, and my few scribbled notes were later undecipherable, so these short paragraphs are only a scant impression of one of the greatest pioneers Great Britain has known.

Thomas Octave Murdoch Sopwith, born in 1888, as his name suggests was the eighth child, but the first son, of a successful civil engineer. He gave his sisters hell and at the age of only eleven took one of them up for her first ride in a hot air balloon. He grew up with fast cars, boats and aeroplanes, being proficient at conducting all of them, and he was one of the first, after Lord Brabazon, to qualify for a British pilot's licence.

At the age of twenty-three he went barnstorming in America, where he met the Wright brothers and another famous name in aviation, Starling Burgess, who was later to design Sopwith's two great adversaries – *Rainbow*, and the all-conquering *Ranger*. He raced both sail and power boats in the States, and got to know their waters intimately, on one occasion taking an unceremonious ducking when his plane stalled off Coney Island and he had to be rescued from the drink. His visit was a great eye-opener for him, and in 1913, only two years later, he founded his own aircraft manufacturing company to build Sopwith 'Pups', 'Snipes' and 'Camels' for the 1914/18 War.

When peace came, Sopwith's company was put into voluntary liquidation, but he immediately started a new aircraft business with his friend Fred Sigrist, naming it after his chief test pilot, an Australian called Harry Hawker. It was because Hawker soon became a giant in British aviation that Sopwith was subsequently able to mount his two costly attacks on the America's Cup.

Tom Sopwith was already recognised as the finest amateur yachtsman in Great Britain, and at the time he decided to take over the reins from Lipton, whose finale he had witnessed in America, he had already won his spurs with his successful 12 Metre *Mouette*. Acquiring *Shamrock V* as a trial horse two years after Lipton's death, he was keen to build another boat and race for the Cup as soon as possible. But King George V felt it might be premature due to the Great Depression, and so Sopwith delayed building his beautiful *Endeavour*, and challenged, through the Royal Yacht Squadron, a season later instead.

Sopwith's memories of 1934, when he came within an ace of winning the Cup, were remarkably clear, but when

I asked him about what he had noted in his photograph album as 'a little luffing incident' (described in the account of that year's match), his mind went blank. '*Ranger*' he said, changing the subject, 'she was the one, she was the boat I could never beat.' But he did defeat Vanderbilt once on that second occasion in 1937. 'I beat him fair and square in a splendid little sailing dinghy called a *Brutal Beast*', he said. 'Did you like Vanderbilt?' I asked him tamely. 'Not always', he replied.

But above all else Tom Sopwith, later knighted for his achievements, must be remembered for one little-known act of philanthropy. At the same time that he was building *Endeavour II*, his technical advisor Frank Murdoch, sent ostensibly to find engines for his new 1,600 ton motor-yacht *Philante*, was having a quiet snoop, in the fine traditions of the Cup, at several European aircraft factories, including Heinkel. It was obvious to him that the Germans were again spoiling for a fight, but although on Murdoch's return Sopwith tried desperately to impress his report on the Government, they felt there was little urgency in bolstering up the country's then insufficient air force. The new Hurricane had been designed by Hawker to be well in advance of Air Ministry specifications, and when they finally agreed to try only a dozen of them, Sopwith, in a fit of frustration, put his hand in his pocket and with his board of directors underwrote four hundred! This incredible act, which, as Murdoch told me, could have cost Sopwith his entire fortune, probably saved England from losing the Battle of Britain and possibly, together with her allies, World War II.

Olin Stephens

Harold Vanderbilt, recognising that his accomplished designer was getting on in years, decided that for his 1937 defender he would ask Starling Burgess to take on an understudy. He wrote: 'In contemplating prospective challenges in the years to come, it seemed that a promising young man should share in the designing work, profit by the experience of the past, and acquire sufficient knowledge to carry on, if need be, single-handed in the future.' Although it was not to be disclosed whose pencil had actually drawn *Ranger*, there is no doubt that her superb lines must have been greatly influenced by his new help, Olin Stephens. Sopwith said of *Ranger*: 'Not only did she beat us anyway, she beat us at the first mark.' And it was this standard that Stephens, one of two great yachting brothers, was to set for over forty years.

Olin Stephens.

Stephens had designed many noteworthy ocean racers and other yachts before he was thirty, and conveniently he was closely associated with the tank-testing facilities at the Stevens Institute of Technology. In all he was to be responsible for the design of six successful Cup defenders: *Ranger* (with Starling Burgess in 1937), *Columbia* (1958), *Constellation* (1964), *Intrepid* (in 1967 and 1970), *Courageous* (1974 and 1977), and *Freedom* in 1980. The only defender he did not design during this period was *Weatherly* (1962), which was drawn by Philip Rhodes.

Apart from *Ranger*, perhaps his most innovative design was *Intrepid*. The product of extensive tank testing, which alone had cost her owners $30,000, she had many unusual features including a separate fin and skeg, a low boom, below-deck winches and a 'bustle'. Many hailed her as a breakthrough but Stephens, in his usual laconic way, said there was no such thing. He held that 'the advancement in 12 Metre design was a cumulative effort by a lot of people to achieve sometimes almost imperceptible improvements in the design of hulls, rigging and sails, which inched forward, one day perhaps, to perfection'. At the time *Intrepid* did not seem to be far off that goal.

Intrepid had reached new standards in high technology and, packaged with her titanium-tipped mast, she had also established new records for the cheque books. Olin Stephens never thought of such horizons, his aim being only to exploit the current rules to the limit, and his talent for getting the best out of a class-boat set an outstanding examples for others to follow.

Emil 'Bus' Mosbacher

Bus Mosbacher, an oil producer and property developer, who had raced sailing yachts since he was a boy, helmed two successful Cup defenders, *Weatherly* in 1962, and the Olin Stephens-designed *Intrepid* in 1967, and had the reputation of being one of the toughest America's Cup skippers of all time. But beneath his rugged exterior there was an unusually subtle mind.

Renowned for his aggressive tactics, Mosbacher also had an extraordinary knack of getting the most out of his boat, controlling it, his crew, and the opposition all at the same time. The opposition in 1962 was formidable, and it had not taken long for the Australians to realise that *Gretel* was the faster yacht. In the second race, Mosbacher, appreciating that they were also getting the best of the tacking duels, broke off the engagement and fooled Jock Sturrock with a long pass, which the Australian skipper lacked the experience to take.

Mosbacher noted that down in his computer-like memory, but this was not the only criticism of the Aussie crew work. Norris Hoyt, who had been giving a commentary on the race, had expressed astonishment that *Gretel*'s crew had failed to make certain adjustments to her sail when reaching, her strongest point of sailing. On hearing about it after winning the race, Mosbacher was furious, and taking Hoyt aside, he told him: 'This is the biggest poker game in the world, and if Jock ever gets a notion that he can beat us on any point of sailing, he might just sail off by himself and do it' Mosbacher was right.

Luckily for Mosbacher, *Intrepid* was a much faster lady. But though there was no longer such physical pressure, the psychological pressure actually increased. The American team had been playing a few games with *Intrepid*'s winches so as to divert attention from her other secrets, and when the Aussies called their bluff and asked for *Intrepid* to be remeasured, Mosbacher, feeling that his old friend Sturrock was accusing him of cheating, let rip. The remeasuring over, and the first race in the bag, Mosbacher sailed straight home and contrary to tradition did not wait for the challenger to finish.

Alan Bond

Alan Bond, born at Ealing near London in 1937, first arrived in Western Australia with his family on the steamer *Himalaya* in January 1950, then aged thirteen. His father had been wounded serving in the Royal Air Force during the war, and he had been informed by his doctors that unless he left England for a warmer climate, he would be dead within two years. If it had not been for Frank Bond's decision to follow the medics' advice, Bondy, as he came to be called, would not have become the winner of the America's Cup and an Australian multi-millionaire.

Fortunately Frank took to the Perth climate well and thrived like his ebullient son, living for a further twenty-one summers. At first Bond did not find it easy to adapt to the Aussie way of life but, leaving his new school after only one year, he soon found he could earn the odd dollar as a sign painter. By 1956, however, certain that he would be better at organising a sign-writing gang than anyone else, he started up his own company, Nu-Signs, which also specialised in cobbling up old houses said to be 'quite beyond repair'. If Bond was told 'you can't do that', he'd already done it, and when he was warned that it was impossible to build houses on precipices, he acquired a hillside for a song, sold lots as fast as he could carve them out, and has carried on singing ever since.

Bond's most famous land deal was the 20,000 acres of rolling desert south of Perth that he named Yanchep Sun City. Even before the grass had grown, he had trees, a golf course and a town centre, and his claim 'where the sun shines ceaselessly' was bringing in buyers from all over the world, attracted by the wide open spaces and eleven miles of white spotless beach.

Bond got into yachting by negotiation, in much the same way. A farmer, interested in buying a corner of his land, asked if he would accept a boat instead of cash, and that was that.

Despite dreadful seasickness, which he eventually overcame like everything else, Bond, who had married at seventeen, fell for sailing as quickly as he had fallen for Eileen, his wife. Wanting something better than *Panamuna*, the farmer's sloop, he sent a man to see Ben Lexcen in Sydney with instructions to design him a 58-footer, and the result was his successful ocean racer *Apollo*, from which he spied his first 12 Metre – and was hooked.

From that moment, Bond went after the Cup as a bear goes after honey. He was under no illusions, it would take a long time, but over four determined challenges the New York bees got increasingly angry and the bear developed a very sore head.

When Bond sailed away with the Cup it was not just honey but plenty of money that he wrapped in a five-dollar note. Lipton may have been the world's best loser, but Bond had no such word in his rich vocabulary. Like Lipton he knew about the power of advertising – the vast assortment of operations controlled by the Bond corporation never being far from his mind. If Lipton was good at selling tea, then Bond having won the cup, was going to sell his beer better.

The bear had one other dream that was to come true, however, and that was to put his sparsely-populated habitat of Western Australia on the map. Oh, for the buzzin' of the bees in those kangaroo trees – it had crossed Bondy's mind that the bees Down Under could be even fiercer!

Ted Turner

The story of how Ted Turner came to win the America's Cup is told later, but why he won it is a different tale.

It could be said that when Ted Turner burst upon the America's Cup scene he was regarded by some as a bit of a clown. Indeed, many conservative East Coast yachtsmen felt that the usurper from Atlanta, Georgia, was about to trample on their toes — as in fact he was.

In many ways Turner's ruthless attitude towards the Cup was similar to that of Alan Bond, who happened to be an old friend from his ocean racing days. Both about the same age, they had each carved out for themselves a considerable fortune, Bond from property and Turner from television, and winning the America's Cup was, do-or-die, their great common objective.

But Turner was different from Bond in two distinct ways: first, he disliked taking risks and, second, he was one of the most accomplished helmsmen in the world. Turner's ocean racing achievements read like a board in a yacht club, only that it would not have fitted in. Making his début in 1966 with his *Vamp X*, he won the Southern Ocean Racing Conference and the Transatlantic Race, before buying the converted 12 Metre *American Eagle*. She was nothing special in modern ocean racing design, but with her Turner won most of the top trophies including the Sydney-Hobart race, both on corrected and elapsed time, the Annapolis-Newport race, and the World Ocean Racing Championships. As if this was not enough, long before he made his bid to defend the America's Cup, he had also taken every 5.5 Metre title in the book. It was no idle jest when, after his failure skippering *Mariner* in the Cup trials of 1964, he had an aeroplane fly over Newport announcing 'MARINER WILL RETURN' – but perhaps for 'Mariner' it should have read 'Turner'.

Turner, flamboyant as he seemed, was a great perfectionist and a student of history. But although once said to have thought of himself as a general in the Civil War, he was no trail-blazer, preferring to carefully count the odds, and get the best, not from a new boat, which he could easily afford, but from a proven winner. He was in that frame of mind when in 1977 he tried to buy the 1974 Cup winner *Courageous*.

Before Turner could act, however, *Courageous* was sold, but it says much for his tenacity (*Tenacious* was another successful boat he owned), that he bought himself a ticket for her helm and, against all the odds, claimed the right to defend. It also said much for his organisational ability that he won the match, to wild acclaim, with a clean sweep. Like Vanderbilt, he had carefully picked the best and most experienced crew, left them to get on with it, and steered his boat unerringly, not by computers, but by the feel fo the wind and the sea. 'I love everybody', he said in carefully measured words afterwards at the press conference, 'everybody in the room'. The 'Mouth from the South' had arrived.

Dennis Conner

If, from those who have won the America's Cup, Turner takes the honours for bravado, then Conner must do the same for sheer dogged determination. As much as Turner had succeeded in ocean racing, Conner had succeeded at match racing. By 1983, having won an Olympic bronze medal in the Tempest Class and twice been world champion of the Star, not to mention countless other conquests, it was natural that as a result of his win as tactician on *Courageous* in 1974, and as helmsman of *Freedom* in 1980, he should be hailed as the finest America's Cup skipper in the business.

Conner, a self-styled 'small town drapery maker', had started sailing as a boy when he joined the San Diego Yacht Club and hitched as many lifts as he could on any boat looking for a crew. Before long he had graduated to ocean racers, and when they started winning, sometimes with Conner at the helm, he adopted sailing almost as his full-time career. Although he was firm, he always handled his team with considerable care, making them feel as important as he was, and 'my guys', as he called his crew, followed him faithfully from race to race. For the 1983 match Conner had men aboard *Liberty* whose Cup experience went back as far as 1958, and his tactician Halsey Herreshoff, grandson of the great designer, was as experienced and as loyal as any.

But Conner's main strength was in his machine-like efficiency and his protracted boat evaluation programmes, which covered hull design, rigging, crews and sails. Herreshoff, whom I was fortunate to meet in America, told me about the crew dedication, as he put it: 'Gone are days when you stopped for lunch. The America's Cup training is now twelve hours a day for three hundred and sixty-five days a year. Sail evaluation, for instance, means endless weeks of racing two boats against each other, making constant sail changes in differing conditions, and taking continuous and tedious measurements until it drives you almost insane.' It was hardly surprising that he had pulled out, at least temporarily after 1983, and for once was hard at work in his office!

Ultimately the test in 1983 was as Conner expected it to be, the worst ordeal of his life. Faced by a faster boat, and psyched by a secret keel, he used all his ingenuity to try and outfox the Australians, and it was only by the smallest agonising margin that he failed. 'There are no excuses,' he said later to the media in Newport, not mentioning the winning crew, '*Australia* was just the better boat on the day.' No man could have tried harder, and the whole world felt for him as with a shallow smile he slipped away down Thames Street before the prize-giving ceremony, and returned home to San Diego to fight another day.

John Bertrand

The Aussie's winged victory in 1983, in John Bertrand's opinion, was not entirely due to their boat. In his book *Born to Win*, he claimed that the *Australia II* tended to wobble downwind and that she was not the rocketship many, and he had always been sceptical, had first expected. Her famous victory was primarily the result of excellent crew work and outstanding seamanship. 'Spit blood!' he had shouted at the winch grinders. 'Spit blood! This is what you were born for!' And as his crew sweated to gain the ascendancy, Bertrand, yelling murder at the 'red boat', had pushed his team to achieve new standards of excellence, and to win the America's Cup, his ultimate life's ambition.

John Bertrand, who had always dreamed of that day, was only seven when he and his brother took delivery of their first eight-foot sailing dinghy, having already spent a summer experimenting with an old flat-bottomed hulk with a parachute that their mother had fashioned for a sail. Subsequently, in a career spanning over thirty years, he had become perhaps the most outstanding helmsman in Australia. After collecting the 'leather medal', for coming fourth in the Finn Dinghy Class of the 1972 Olympics, he went on to win the 'bronze' in 1976, and would have represented Australia again in the Soling Class in 1980 if the team had not been withdrawn as a protest against the Russian invasion of Afghanistan. Bertrand had also been on *Gretel II* when, in his opinion, she had rightly been disqualified in the second race of the 1970 series, and it was only natural that Alan Bond, having persuaded him to crew also on *Southern Cross* in 1974 and on *Australia* in 1980, had immediately appointed him skipper for 1983.

From that moment on, the thirty-seven-year-old John Bertrand was dedicated to winning, and between *Australia II*'s launching in June 1982 and the final day of reckoning in Newport, he was to race her against various boats almost three hundred times. Having at the age of twenty-two gained a degree in Mechanical engineering at Melbourne's Monash University, and since then acquired the Melbourne franchise for North Sails, Bertrand was well-qualified to take the challenger through her trials and his message to his crew was quite simple: 'We are going to attain a standard that will put us not only in front of the Americans but twenty years ahead.'

On the fifth leg of that last spine-chilling race, when Bertrand, trailing 45 seconds behind Conner, found a breeze and sailed past him, it is worth recording the words of Hughey Treharne, his tactician, as the winches whirred and *Liberty* gybed across the course to try and stop them. 'Here she comes, John', he yelled, and then as Bertrand forged on, knowing that his boat would be disqualified if they so much as touched, 'She takes our stern', John, she takes our stern!' It was the moment of truth, and as 500 million people watching from all over the world held their breaths, the cool professional Bertrand, as he wrote later in his book, heard *Liberty*'s light bow wave as she slid by behind them.

Sir Peter Blake OBE

'Sailing offers everything: physical exercise, mental recreation and a chance to relax', wrote Peter Blake in his book *An Introduction to Sailing* (David Bateman Ltd, 1993). If there was any sailor alive never relaxed in a boat, it was Peter Blake.

When New Zealand won the America's Cup in May 1995, Peter Blake, their charismatic team leader, whose bright red socks had been copied for good luck by almost the entire country, immediately disclosed plans for a one-boat defence. With a total population of just 3.8 million, there was no way that they could afford the costs likely to be incurred by many of the challengers for the America's Cup 2000. Blake was right. By the time the Cup came round again, Prada, the Italian challenge, for example, was reputed to have raised a cool US$70 million.

But what the Kiwis lacked in hard cash they made up for in determination. Peter Blake, who in 1995, had fired up Team New Zealand with the same indomitable spirit as Sir Michael Fay, the New Zealand financier, had during and since the 1987 contest, made it quite clear. 'We don't need to go on a spending spree, we just need to win races.' His plan was realistic. Paul Cayard, the rising American star of match racing, had said of the Team New Zealand underdogs in 1995: 'You are witnessing the best performance by any challenger in the recent history of the America's Cup.'

Peter Blake breathed performance. New Zealanders are ferocious opponents at the best of times, but with his organisational skills now behind the 2000 defence, they looked unbeatable. Born in Auckland, Peter started racing dinghies as a boy and built his own boat. But his great love became ocean racing, first as master of the famous maxi *Heath's Condor* and later taking part in five Whitbread Round the World Races, culminating in his famous victory with *Steinlager 2*.

Such was the respect of his team, that their concentration on winning the Cup for a second time was astonishing and it was partly due to his leadership that *Black Magic* crushed her Italian opponent as easily as a shark would a seal.

Shortly after his second America's Cup victory, Sir Peter decided to retire from yacht racing and to concentrate his formidable skills on the world of ecology and preserving the environment. In 2001, soon after he had dropped anchor in the mouth of the Amazon, his yacht was boarded by pirates, who threatened his crew with their lives. In the ensuing melée Peter Blake was shot dead. Never since the days of cannon has the loss of such a great sailor been mourned.

Russell Coutts

Hardly had Russell Coutts steered *Black Magic* to win the America's Cup in 2000 than the head hunters were hounding around him for 2003. Finance was always a problem for Team New Zealand and now with his great mentor Peter Blake retired from battle, Russell Coutts, together with his eminent tactician Brad Butterworth and four other leading crew members, decided to jump ship and join billionaire Ernesto Bertarelli's *Alinghi* challenge. Thus, having talked of defending the Cup for his country for '100 years', Coutts was soon to endure the vitriol of many of his previous supporters.

Once on target, however, Coutts' determination to succeed carries all before the mast. Brushing aside the flak from his compatriots, his masterly win with *Alinghi* in 2003 established him as the finest helmsman in the Cup's history – overtaking both Charlie Barr, the American skipper, who won nine races during the 1899, 1901 and 1903 regattas, and more recently the legendary Dennis Conner.

It all began, as with many outstanding sailors, racing dinghies. During the 1984 Olympic Games, while suffering from a painful boil on his backside, which would have caused many to throw in the towel, Coutts won the gold medal in the Finn class. Later, in 1986, he was to crew on Michael Fay's 'plastic fantastic' in the first New Zealand challenge off Fremantle, Western Australia, before, surprisingly, heading back to university to complete a degree in engineering.

The degree held him in good stead and his understanding of the forces that make a yacht work later proved invaluable. By the early 1990s his focus had turned to match racing, where two boats compete against each other on straight upwind and downwind courses. Fighting his corner around the world by 1996 he had won 20 Grade 1 match races against very tough opposition. For 35 months he reigned supreme and during the period he won the world match racing championship no less than three times.

But Coutts' greatest achievements have been in the America's Cup. Yet when he looked set for another win in 2007, due to a presumed clash of personalities with *Alinghi*'s Ernesto Bertarelli, and despite a last ditch attempt at reconciliation, he was left without a boat. A man of such a ferocious temperament cannot be held down for long, and after he had spent time developing his own RC44 match racer and creating a World Sailing League – racing state of the art 70 foot (21 metre) catamarans – his fellow New Zealanders, forgiving him for everything, wanted him back.

THE 'LADIES'

I've taken my fun where I've found it,
An' now I must pay for my fun,
For the more you 'ave known o' the others
The less will you settle to one …
　　'The Ladies', Rudyard Kipling

If the ladies had become too expensive between the wars, they were only mere shadows of those that came thereafter. No longer content with building a single challenger, clubs were soon expecting to pick the best of several, and today it takes millions to mount an attack on the America's Cup — compared with the total of £5,000 it once cost England to defeat the might of the Spanish Armada!

What mad impulse urges gentlemen to spend these vast and escalating sums on such timeworn ladies often defies the imagination, but not that of their designers. Olin Stephens may well have said that there was no longer any such thing as a breakthrough in 12 Metre design, but many, now using expensive computerised techniques, are still trying very hard to achieve it.

The America's Cup is not just a saga of the sea, therefore, but also a study of length, sail area and displacement, and the magic formula that year after year gets these ladies to lift their skirts a little higher and to travel just a little bit faster: not easy to depict in a painting, but the subject of several of those reproduced in this book.

'The evolution of yacht design,' wrote an American naval historian in 1935, 'has not been a logical steady series of improvements.' Indeed, from the time that the yacht *America* first went on the stocks in 1851, the design of the Cup boats has been a history of fits and starts and discarded plans.

America herself was the result of competition, for she was based on the design of the pilot boats that used to race out to meet the ships entering New York harbour. Built first as a model, she was then marked out on the floor with battens by her designer George Steers, before timbers were cut to match them. It was not exactly trial and error, but something very close to it, and her clean lines were to become the envy of many British yachtsmen who had little idea of how to copy her, although her sharp clipper bow was to be a feature of *Livonia* in 1871 and *Thistle* in 1887, but surprisingly not that of *Genesta* between them.

The year 1885 had seen the culmination of two very different concepts pursued on opposite sides of the Atlantic. For many years the British were convinced that a narrow hull gave greater speed and a deep keel better stability, but the Americans were equally certain that a centreboard was better, lowered through a shallow flat hull, which could skim faster through the water. The variants, which in time came to be known as the 'plank on edge' or 'skimming dish' designs each had their advantages, but inevitably by the end of that

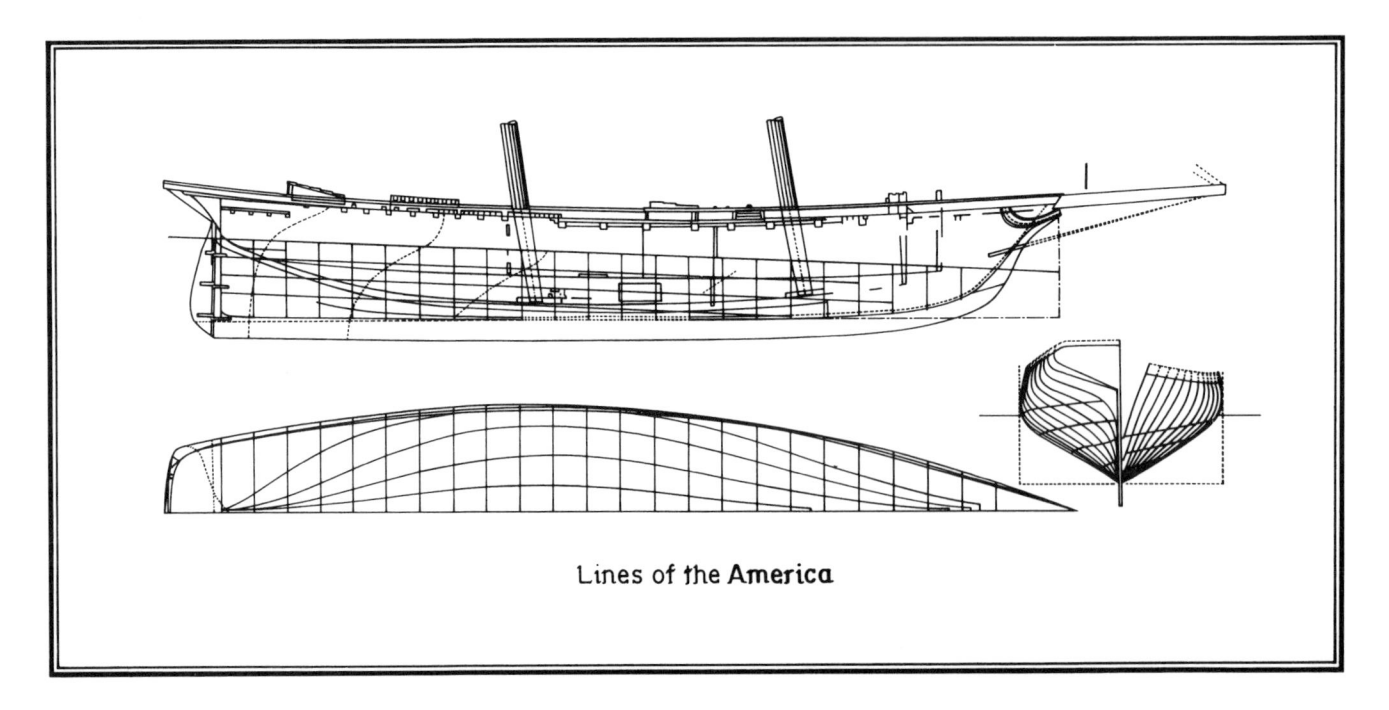

Lines of the **America**

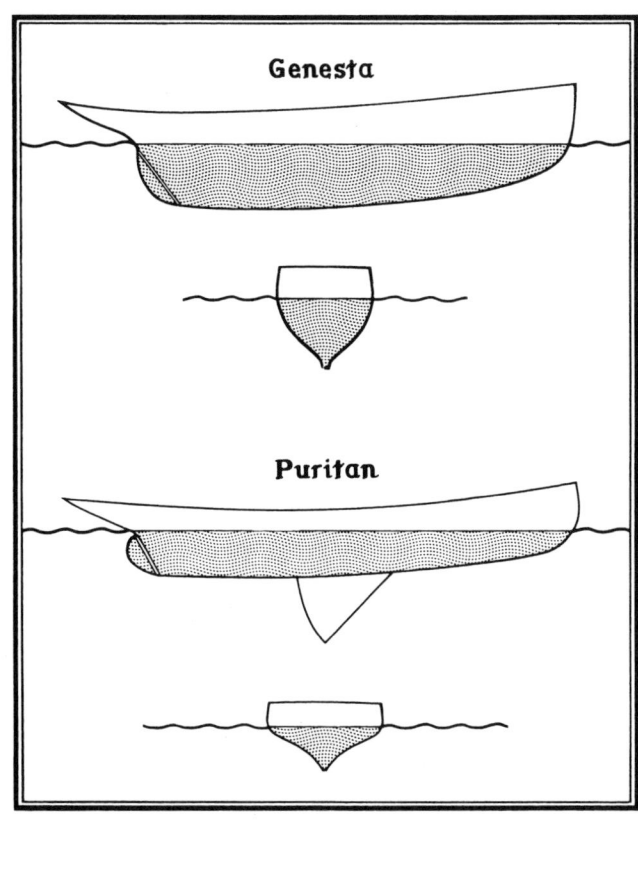

decade such extremes had been largely abandoned, and the lines had come closer together.

In 1887 the rules were amended by the New York Yacht Club to limit the water-line length of competing boats to 90 foot (27.5 metre), but as the official measurement was taken when the boat was on an even keel it gave designers, for the first time, plenty of reason to experiment with new and more advanced ideas. The speed of a boat being directly proportional to the square root of the length of the water-line, it was apparent that by lengthening the overhangs at both ends the yachts would sail faster when heeled over in a breeze. Also, as displacement had not been greatly penalised (which favoured the shallower draft American vessels), it meant that large areas of the keel could be dispensed with, thus reducing the drag of surplus wetted surface at the expense of additional slabs of lead.

It is interesting to compare the line drawings in this book, so beautifully executed by Ethan Danielson, and from them to see the evolution of the racing yacht of today. As keels became deeper, sometimes complemented by a centreboard, masts became progressively taller, until in 1903 *Reliance* carried a rig which soared 196 foot (60 metres) into the air. In 1881 the schooner rig had changed to gaff-rigged cutter, finally becoming the high aspect ratio bermudian rig of 1934, which has been successfully used on most great racing boats, including the much smaller 12 Metres, with a few variations right up to present times.

During the earlier Cup races, sail area increased enormously, and it was not until *Reliance*, with her flat

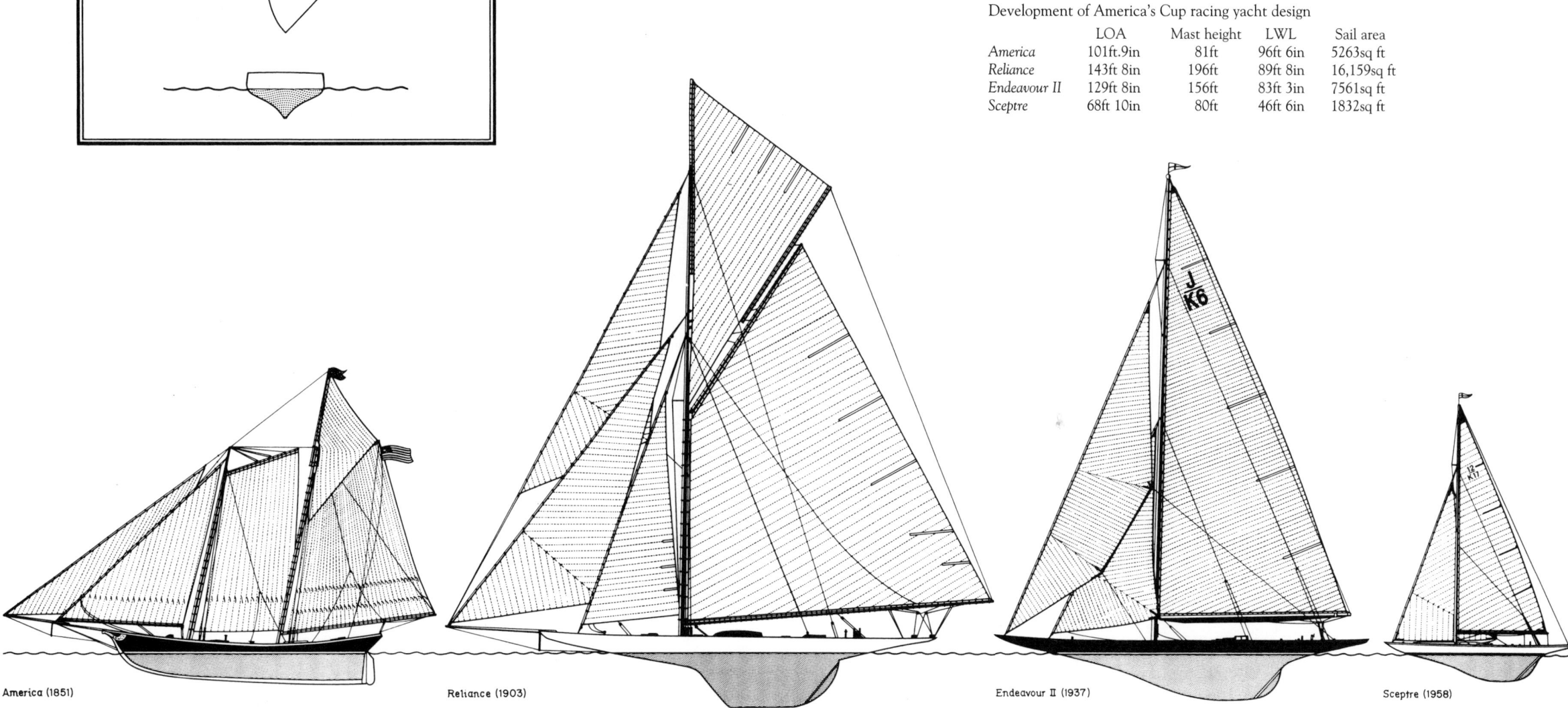

Development of America's Cup racing yacht design

	LOA	Mast height	LWL	Sail area
America	101ft.9in	81ft	96ft 6in	5263sq ft
Reliance	143ft 8in	196ft	89ft 8in	16,159sq ft
Endeavour II	129ft 8in	156ft	83ft 3in	7561sq ft
Sceptre	68ft 10in	80ft	46ft 6in	1832sq ft

displacement hull, proved almost totally unseaworthy, that much was done to restrict it. It is interesting to note that from the tip of her bowsprit to the end of her boom *Reliance's* length was the same as her height, and her immense spread of 16,159 square foot (1,502 square metre) made her look like some magnificent butterfly carried along on the wind. But sadly, like a butterfly she quickly died, reduced to scrap only two months after winning the Cup, and it was obvious that such appalling wastage had to stop.

Handling tons of canvas called for many innovations in equipment, and amongst other clever Herreshoff inventions *Reliance* had a telescopic topmast, which died with her, and fair-leads taking sheets and halyards to nine two-speed winches situated below her deck. This latter idea was again used on *Enterprise* in 1930, and by Olin Stephens with *Intrepid* in 1967 as shown in the painting of that year. When the Universal Rule was introduced for the 1930 match, ensuring that yachts in future raced as one class without handicap, the Americans again scored a first by fitting *Enterprise* with an alloy mast which gave her a significant weight advantage over her British rival.

Sail material, which was once extremely heavy, has also altered dramatically since those early days, but it is interesting that from the moment that the yacht *America* was first sighted off the English coast with sails like boards, the Yankees have rarely ceased to hold the lead. The billowing British sails at that time tended to be made of loosely hand-woven flax which had to be constantly doused with water in order to trap the wind, but the *America's* sails were made of machine-spun cotton duck which not only stretched as tight as a drum but also was of far less weight. Later Herreshoff scored another first by producing cross-cut sails, which were cut on the bias, and in 1958 the Americans were the first to try, with excellent results, the new synthetic Dupont material, Dacron. It was not long before they banned any challenger from using it, but meanwhile ICI had developed Terylene, which after a time became generally accepted as a suitable alternative until Kevlar was introduced again by the Americans in 1974, causing Alan Bond to boil over when he failed to stop them using it, or worse still to obtain it himself! The more recent Kevlar/Mylar sails, which glow like striped gold in the sunlight, are not cheap, and a locker of, say, fifty sails now absorbs a major slice of any budget.

One sail that caused a great stir in the 1930s was the quadrilateral or double-clewed jib, first flown by *Endeavour* in 1934. It had not gone unnoticed by the opposition, and before she arrived in America it had already been copied – although it has never again become fashionable, like the Park Avenue boom and so many other ideas. The 'J's' were also responsible for the parachute spinnakers, known in England as 'Annie Oakleys' (as they seemed to be shot full of holes), and in America, due to their volume, somewhat obviously as 'Mae Wests' *Ranger* was subsequently equipped with one of 18,000 square foot (1,670 square metre), the largest sail ever made. In 1958 *Sceptre* also carried a huge spinnaker, fashioned by a Frenchman called Jean-Jacques Herbulot, but it was often no match for the smaller balloon spinnakers that had meanwhile evolved, and proved no more successful than any other of her features, including the forward shape of her hull.

The paintings of the British challenges in 1958 and 1964, show how easy it is to get the design of a 12 Metre hopelessly wrong. Frank Murdoch described for me the ceaseless ocean under-swell off Newport, and how often British designers tended to forget it. Apparently the natural period of pitching is linked to the given longitudinal moment of a yacht's inertia but this can be greatly influenced by weight distribution and hull shape, as any pitching entrains movement of a greater or lesser mass of water with it. This is important as it affects the damping of the pitching motion, which if too severe, as in the case of both *Sceptre* and *Sovereign*, creates loss of drive from the sails which in turn creates increased hobby-horsing. Although this aspect of yacht design had never been understood, it was why the later 'Twelves' tended to have fine deep forward sections changing to flatter afterbodies. It was important that the artist, Tim Thompson, understood such details before he put brush to canvas and the scene moved on to the new America's Cup Class, introduced in 1992.

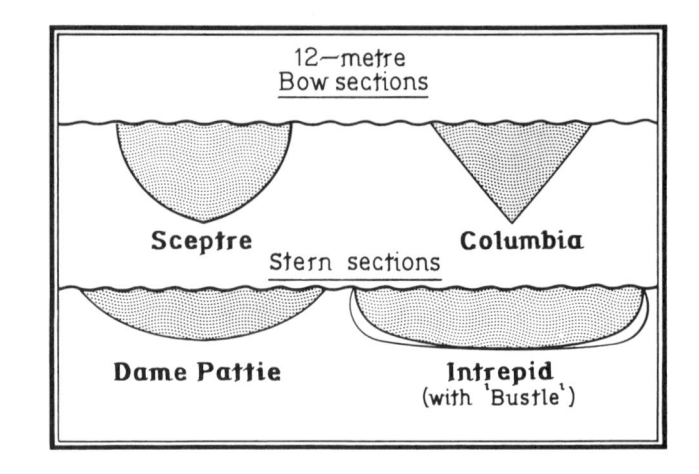

THE COURSES

Cowes, Isle of Wight

The crowds gathering on the Cowes waterfront in 1851 were not large by today's standards, for it was before, but not long before, yacht racing as a spectator sport became popular. It was not until the following decade, when the Prince of Wales, later to become King Edward VII, started visiting Cowes for the Royal Yacht Squadron's annual August Regatta, that this small rambling seaport on the Isle of Wight, already the mecca of British yachting, became properly established. However, stories about the yacht *America* had spread far and wide, and as *The Times* stated:

There must have been upwards of 100 yachts lying at anchor in the Roads, the beach was crowded from Egypt Point to the piers, the Esplanade in front of the club thronged with gentlemen and ladies. Booths were erected all along the quay, and the roadstead was alive with boats, while from the sea and shore rose an incessant buzz of voices, mingled with the splashing of oars, the flapping of sails, and the hissing of steam from the excursion vessels preparing to accompany the race.

Although Cowes would not necessarily be suitable for an America's Cup course today, Torbay for example being better, the race scheduled to be 'round the Isle of Wight, inside Nomansland buoy and Sandhead buoy, and outside the *Nab*' seemed appropriate at the time, particularly as the home fleet had a greater understanding of the complex tidal flows that prevailed.

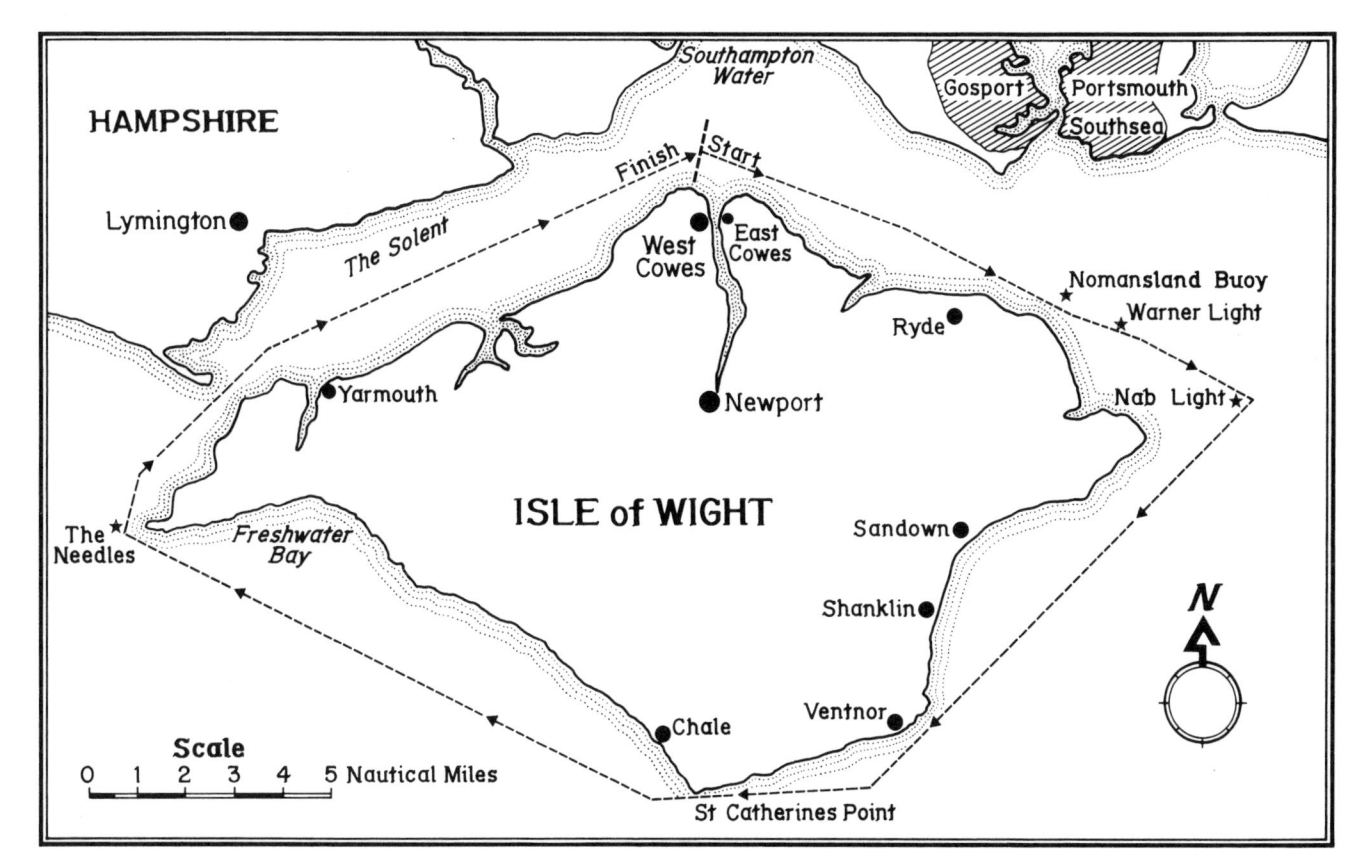

Royal Yacht Squadron Course 1851

The fact that *America* passed inside the *Nab*, thus probably saving herself two miles, was an oversight that we have all been inclined to forget — until Tim Thompson, I believe for the first time, dared to put this surprising event on canvas.

New York Yacht Club — Inside Course

The New York Yacht Club, formed in 1844, established two race courses south of the city at the approaches to the harbour. The inside sheltered course, starting just below Tompkinsville, ran past the original clubhouse on the shores of Staten Island and down through the narrows between two forts, Fort Hamilton to the east being close to the extremities of Long Island. It was then flagged on southwards through the Chapel Hill channel, before it swung east to the *Sandy Hook* light vessel, from whence the yachts returned. With its shoals and currents it was almost as tricky as that round the Isle of Wight, and local knowledge was again invaluable.

A report from the *Field* in 1870, describing the first challenge for the America's Cup, stated:

The river was crowded with steamboats, who never seemed tired of steaming around us, with their whistles shrieking by way of salutation, and their crowds of spectators shouting Hooray. There were bands too which played God Save the Queen and Yankee Doodle – but what concerned us was to know where all these steamboats, some of them huge river boats with 300 people on board, would be when the yachts were under way beating through the Narrows.

It was for this reason that the inside course, which had always put the American 'skimming dishes' at a definite advantage, was finally abandoned in 1887. The painting of *Thistle* in that year vividly evokes the atmosphere of those early matches.

New York Yacht Club – Outside Course

The outside course was arranged so that it was instantly available when inshore racing became impossible through lack of wind. Most matches were staged to combine both courses, however, and frequently the outside course, as seen in the painting of the last match held there in 1920, tested the yachts as if they were out in the open sea. From the *Sandy Hook* or *Scotland* light vessels a triangular course could be laid out in most directions for the prevailing conditions on a 10 mile

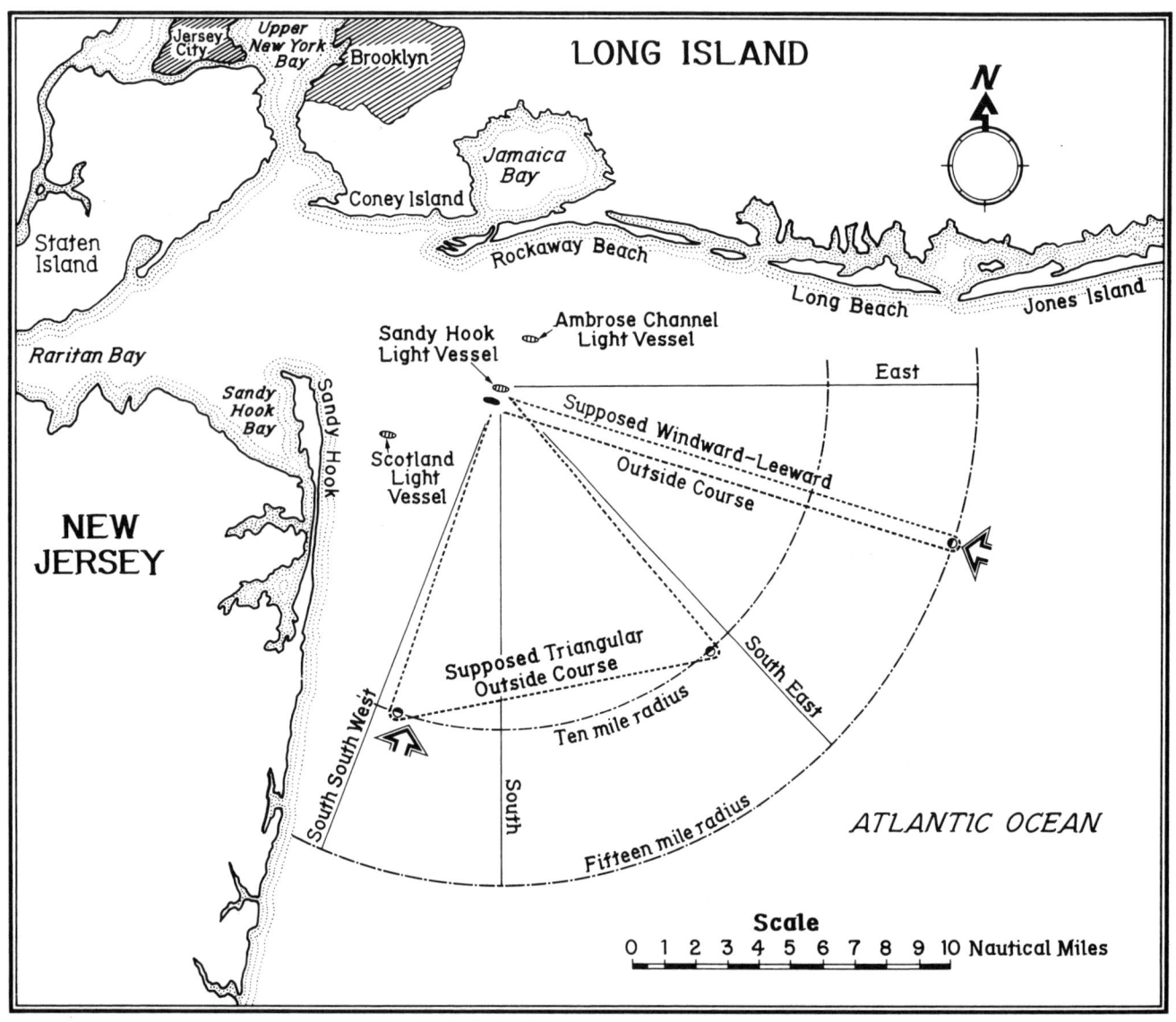

New York Yacht Club Course (Inside) 1870-1920

New York Yacht Club Course (Outside) 1870-1920

(16 km) radius, or when a windward-leeward course was required, on a 15 mile (24 km) or 20 mile (32 km) radius. It was on such a course somewhere south of Long Beach, shown in our diagram drawn from an 1871 press cutting, that *Livonia* made her fatal blunder, as illustrated later, of passing the stake-boat on the wrong hand, thereby gibing and consequently losing the race.

Before the 1930 series the New York course had become so choked by flotsam, and the growing number of would-be spectator craft, that 'Mike' Vanderbilt ordered a study to be made of an alternative course off Newport, Rhode Island – another reason being that *Enterprise*'s 162 foot (50 metre) 'tin mast' would not fit under many of the East River bridges. Previously Sir Thomas Lipton, *Shamrock*'s owner, had resisted this change, for as he had once said about advertising, 'when a duck lays an egg, she makes no' a sound. An' how many people eat ducks' eggs?' He finally accepted, but only reluctantly, as he much preferred the cackle of the hens in New York's front yard!

Newport, Rhode Island
When the America's Cup circus arrived in Newport, some time after the Navy had left, it was much the same as any other small New England holiday town – but not for long. Although there was to be a brief respite during World War II, the Cup brought its own special calling card, and mansions soon became crew dormitories, streets became traffic jams and the toy shops became America's Cup museums. Behind the Black Pearl saloon the jetties became the playground for some of the most celebrated yachtsmen in the world and there, visible until October 1983, lay the shark-like silhouettes of the 12 Metres, constantly under preparation for sea. It was an idyllic setting for a race, which over the years had become increasingly famous, and the open waters south of Sakonnet Point were, in many ways, a spectator's ideal stage and a skipper's perfect paradise.

During racing, and once each day's weather pattern had been fully assimilated, the course would be chosen and signalled by the committee boat. It would then be marked out from the *America's Cup* buoy, shown in the painting of the 1937 match – which acted for both start and finish. Before the war the 'J's were asked to race 30 miles (48 km), and afterwards the 'Twelves' a distance of 24 miles (39 km), and all courses could be set, depending on the wind, in any conceivable direction. However, by 1964 tastes had altered.

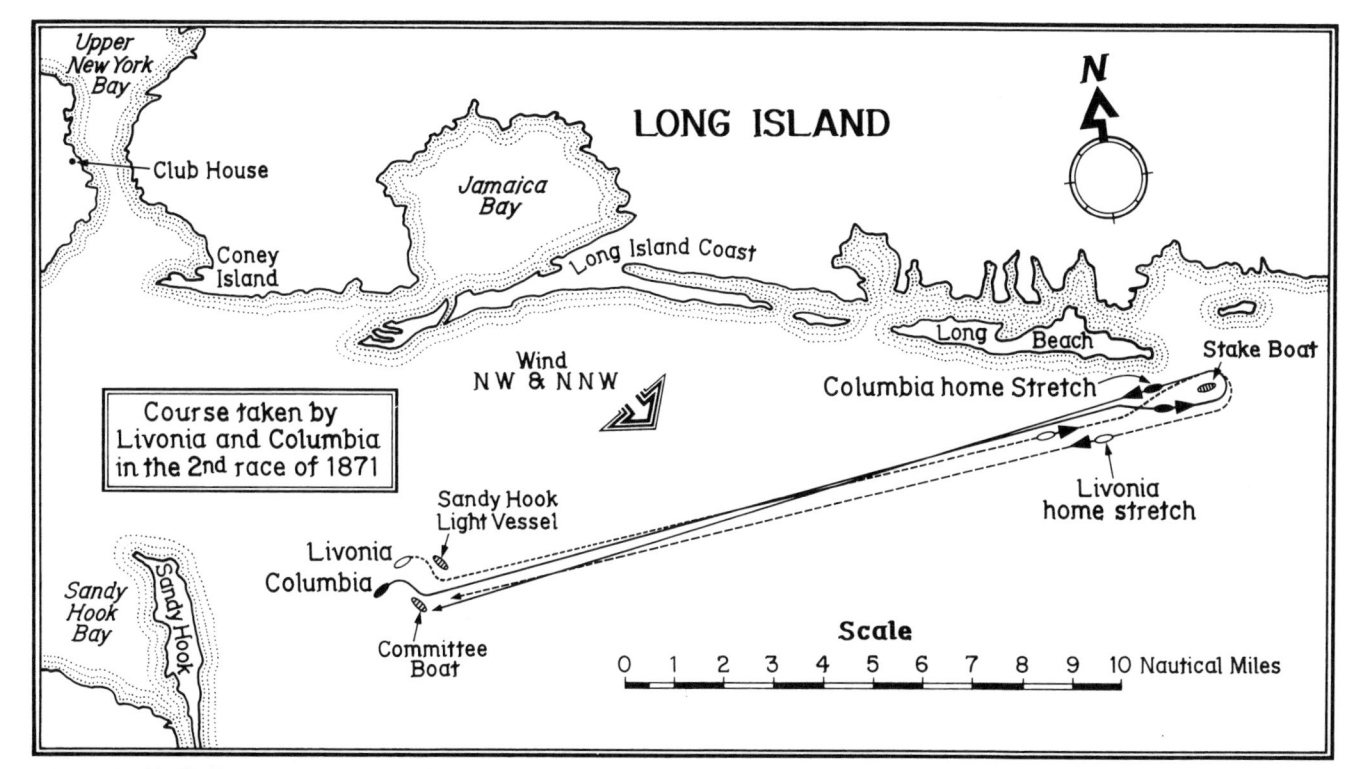

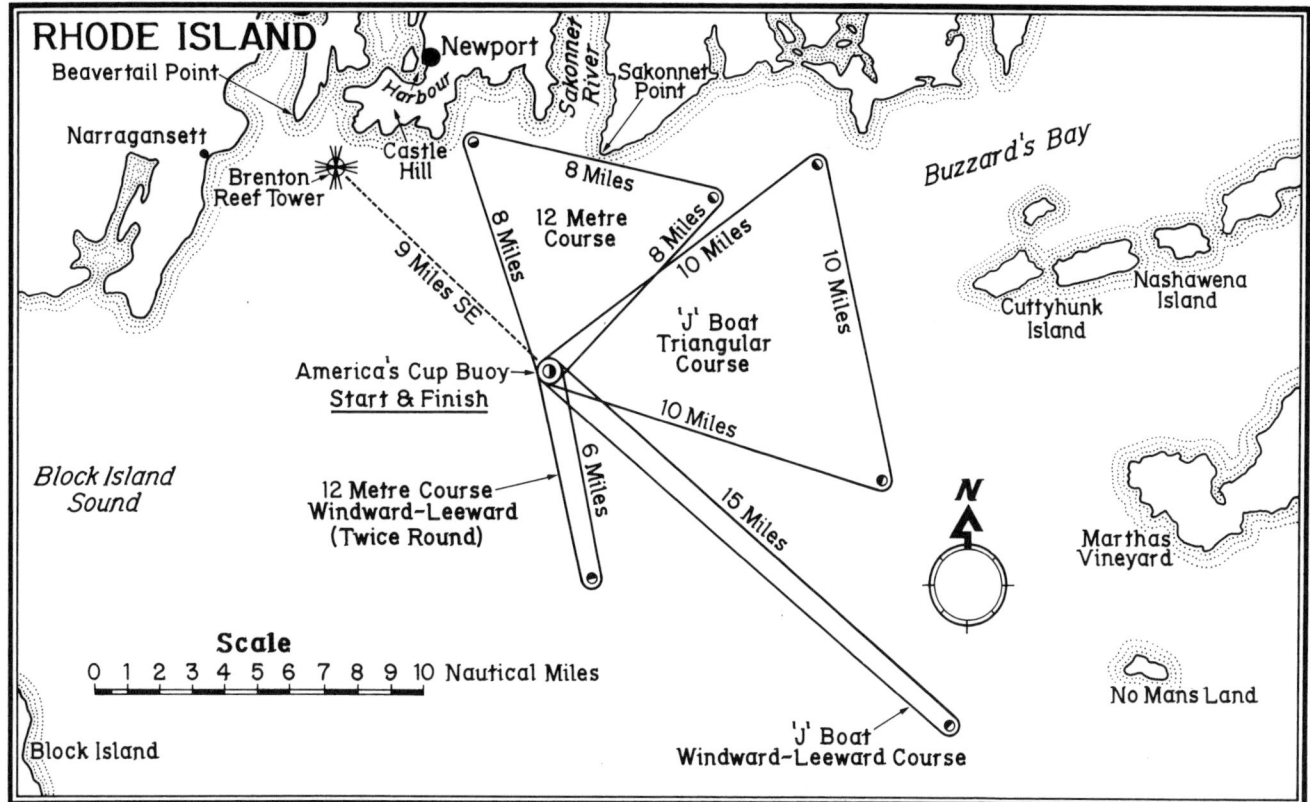

America's Cup Course 1930-1962

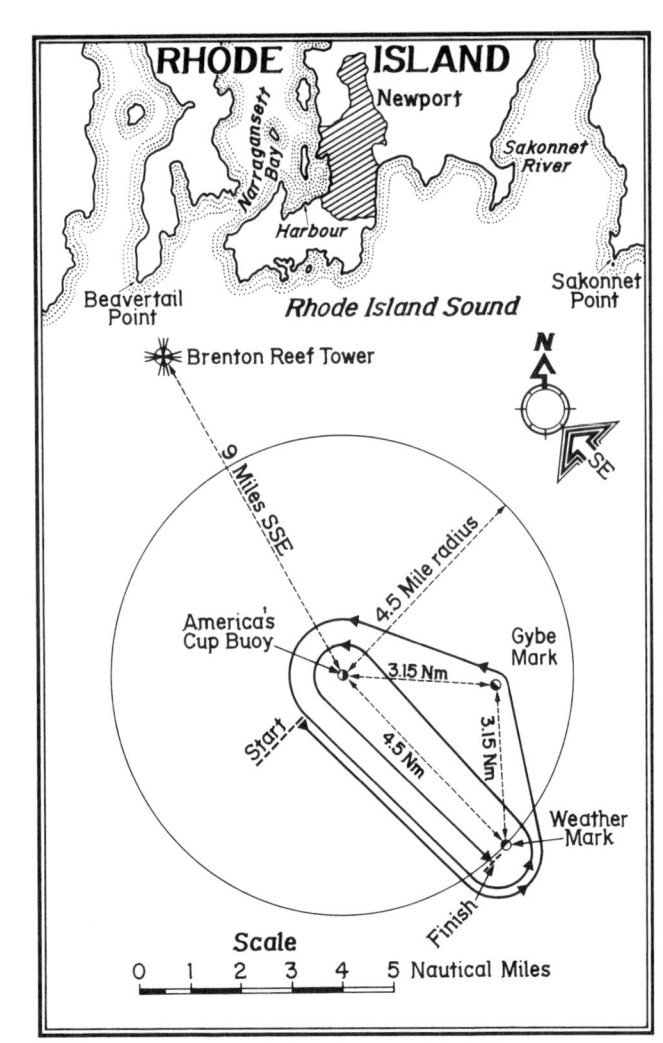

We have attempted to convey the thrill of this in some of the latter paintings of the 12 Metres. However, nothing could now describe the poignancy of that rusting *America's Cup* buoy, waiting interminably for further days of glory, and tossing restlessly – alone on the Newport chop.

Perth
On 30 October 1983, 900,000 people turned out in Perth to welcome back their heroic crew to the wildest acclaim. It was a victory that had stopped the hearts of a whole nation, and as Alan Bond had always envisaged, not only had it put Western Australia in the headlines more than most had ever dreamt of, but it would give the Cup a new meaning, demonstrated later when a record fourteen entries were received by the Royal Perth Yacht Club for 1987. If the Cup had to change hands, it could not have gone to a better home. Bathed in more sunshine than any other Australian capital, and pounded by the crashing surf of the Indian Ocean, Perth, with its comparatively tiny population, is a very beautiful place.

Soon after they had won the Cup, the Royal Perth Yacht Club set up a management committee to design an even tighter and more demanding course for their defence, and to arrange the necessary back-up facilities at Fremantle (or 'Freo'), 11 miles (15 km) downstream on the banks of the Swan River. From the club, perched on the edge of sparkling Matilda Bay, new marinas were conjured up, and accommodation to house, it seemed, the whole of the world of yachting.

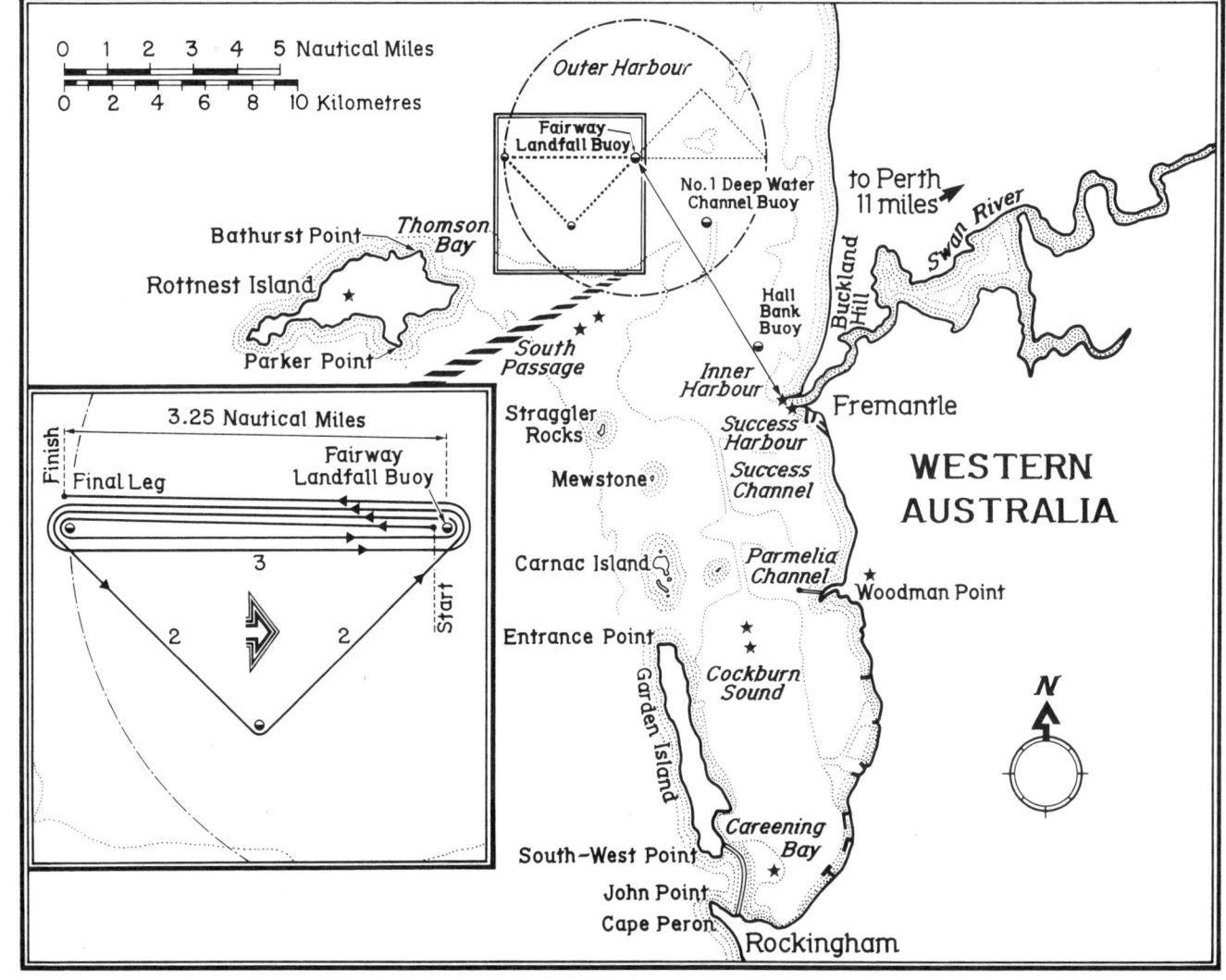

America's Cup Course 1964-1983

Newport — Revised Course, 1964
The close contest of 1962 had stimulated great enthusiasm in the United States, and one of the results was that the New York Yacht Club decided to abandon the traditionally alternating triangular and windward-leeward courses in favour of making the America's Cup matches more of a challenge.

Gretel had proved far too fast downwind for the Americans' liking, and so, partly in order to even out such disadvantages, it was decided to adopt the shorter legs of the single Olympic course instead. The new course combined all the hazards of the previous ones, except that everything happened an awful lot faster, and it was primarily responsible for the tack-gybe spinnaker sets and the other slick manoeuvres that have made match racing the better and more exciting sport it is today.

America's Cup Course 1987

But no such reception was planned by the winds that often sweep inshore in their afternoon rush for the Australian desert. Few crews had yet experienced the wild seas and the lashing spray loved by the Aussies, and so generously meted out by their notorious friend — the 'Fremantle Doctor'.

San Diego
After the 1987 America's Cup in Perth, Dennis Conner, the winner, appeared to hold most of the cards. There was much speculation as to where the next cup was to be staged, and rumour ranged from the Bay of Mexico to the stormy waters off Hawaii, where Conner had trained for the 1987 match, and where he had apparently struck up a good relationship with the local 'yachties'.

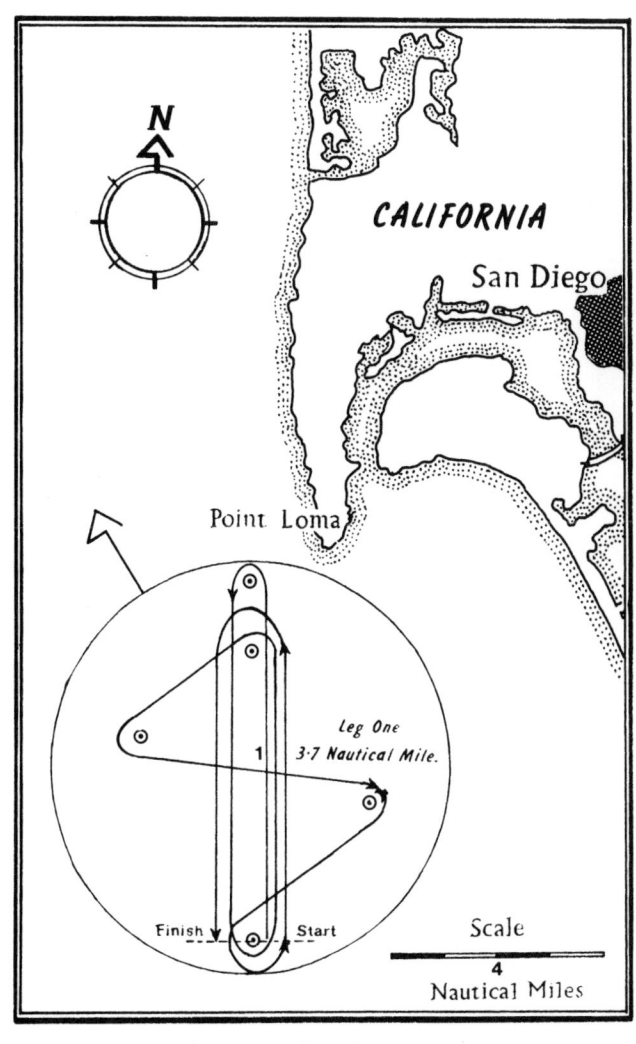

But it was not to be. The San Diego Yacht Club soon showed their hand of aces and Conner, having been brought to heel, was instructed to defend the Cup in the sloppy waters he knew best off the coast of Southern California. Little did he expect to be dodging kelp (seaweed) beds off point Loma in a catamaran as he raced the giant New Zealand 'K' boat the very next year.

In 1992 a Cup course was laid off Point Loma which was to create the most slam-bam action for both crews and spectators in any America's Cup yet. Consisting of several 'hairpins' it kept the 'coffee grinders' from the coffee and also gave the spinnaker trimmer plenty of work by re-introducing, for the first time in recent Cup history, a downwind finish. This had the effect of making it easier for the trailing yacht to steal the leading yacht's wind and thus catch up. But even this failed to arouse much enthusiasm, from either the spectators or the media, and on shore the America's Cup Museum remained half-empty.

In the end, the vast and sprawling city of San Diego, despite one further chance in 1995 to stage a more enthralling event, could never complete with the more intimate atmosphere of Newport, Rhode Island, Fremantle or Cowes, and for most competitors the location never really appealed.

Auckland
Tuesday 23 November
Calm or light airs from the northward. Some of the officers went ashore to amuse themselves among the natives, where they saw the head and bowels of a youth that had been lately killed. A piece of flesh had been broiled and eaten in their presence casing them to vomit.

Captain James Cook, New Zealand, 1770

Visitors to Auckland now do not find the natives quite so hungry! New Zealand has come a long way since those early days and in May 1995, the Kiwis were well satisfied that, after a decade of trying to win the America's Cup, their economy, and their boating industry, looked like taking off again, with the cup at last in their locker. Meanwhile, speculators waited eagerly to cash in on the properties they had previously purchased along the magnificent Auckland waterfront.

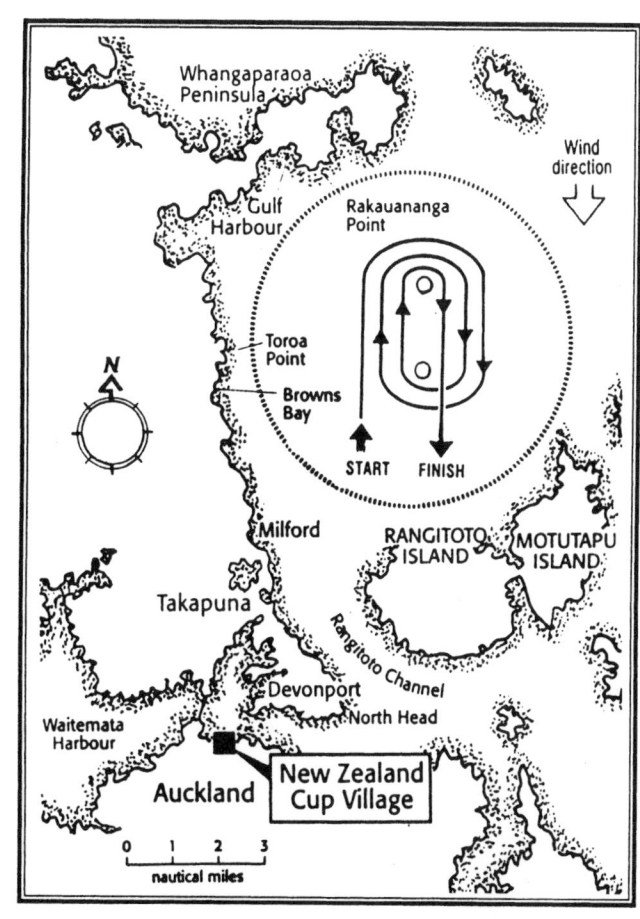

New Zealand, with its small but determined

America's Cup Course 1992

America's Cup Course 1995–2003

population, now seems to shine at all team sports: nowhere in the world is there a nation more fired up by sailing, and no country, to date has been more successful. The preparations for the America's Cup 2000 were as thorough, if not more so, as if they were preparing for the Olympic Games.

Defending the Cup has never been easy and improvements in information technology have done little to boost home crew confidence. While the challengers fine-tune their yachts through competition, defenders can only pray that they have a winner.

In 2003 Team New Zealand faced not only crippling defections but also the best prepared and financed fleet in America's Cup history. They had only one card left to play, the technological one. But when the 'Hula' skirt, which added length and hopefully speed to their boat, failed to impress and super-light spars started to shatter, it was largely technology that let them down.

Valencia

Flying into Valencia, a city situated half way down the Mediterranean coast of Spain, one is struck by the long curving beach bisected by twin harbour entrances with myriads of sprawling buildings, including an obvious new arts complex, stretching far into the distance behind. To seaward could be seen a vast spectator fleet spread out in diamond formation around a race course.

As the America's Cup itself has become increasingly sophisticated, the Cup's courses have become less so. Indeed courses, where once yachts had to zig-zag between marks set to make life difficult, now comply so strictly with standard match racing rules, that only the weather conditions add an element of uncertainty.

At Valencia winds were forecast to blow, mainly onshore, at speeds varying from between 10-15 knots during June to 12-20 knots during July, with sea conditions expected to remain reasonably calm. Two courses were designated close to the coast. 'Romeo', the northern course, used for the Louis Vuitton semi-finals and finals and the Cup itself, was off the America's Cup port entrance, and 'Juliet' the southern course was to the far side of Valencia's adjoining commercial port entrance.

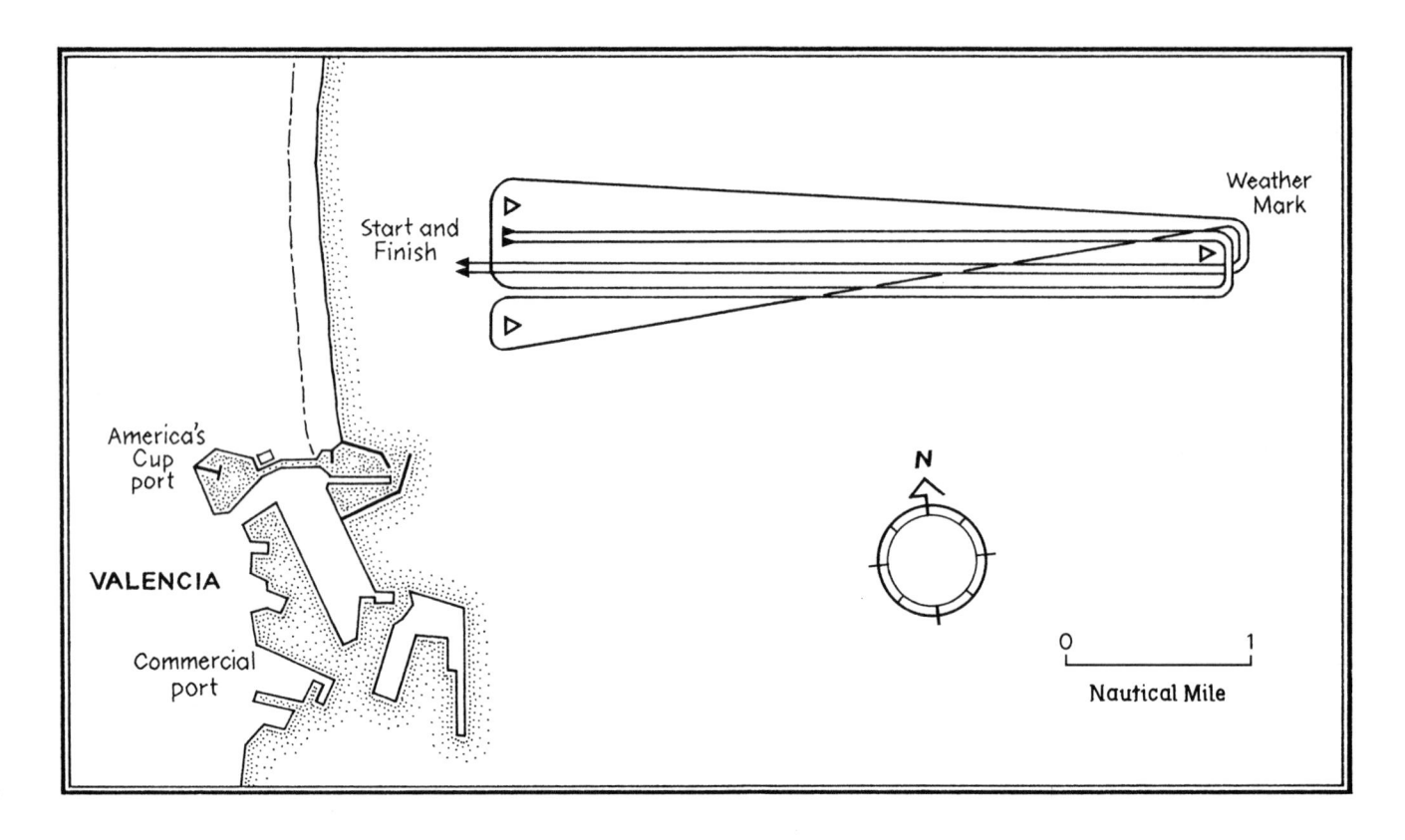

THE INTERNATIONAL AMERICA'S CUP CLASS

After nearly 30 years racing, the last 12 Metre class yachts – first launched in 1907 but not introduced to the Cup until 1958 – sailed across the line for the last time at Fremantle, Western Australia, in 1987. Even Michael Fay's last-ditch attempt to upgrade the old war-horses by introducing fibreglass construction came too late.

1992 saw the debut of the innovative International America's Cup Class (IACC) yachts designed to take advantage of the latest space-age technology, and the fact that they were radically different from their eighty-year-old forebears was hardly surprising. The use of carbon fibre was now permitted in the construction of both masts and hulls and the resulting craft were both lighter and, with a greater sail area, faster than the previous class of yachts. The new rules also allowed a heavier boat to carry more sail, and with relatively few restrictions on beam and underwater configuration, they gave designers plenty of scope. The crew of sixteen – smaller than might be expected for such a large sail area – made the boats suitably 'hot to handle'.

Crewing an IACC yacht
1 Observer One 'non-executive' place is kept for the owner or his nominee; on early racing days this might be one of the designers.
2 Helmsman The most important member of the crew (who may also be the skipper). Steers the yacht with one of two wheels, often giving tacking and sail-changing orders.
3 Tactician Responsible for most tactical race decisions, reached on the basis of wind and sea conditions and the relative positions, strengths and likely strategy of the opposition.
4 Navigator Plots the optimum course between marker buoys using a sophisticated array of wind direction and speed instruments, together with satellite navigation displays and weather data.
5 Mainsheet Trimmer Adjusts the shape of the mainsail, tensioning the mainsheet on the winch with the traveller positioning the boom correctly over the boat.
6 & 7 Headsail Trimmers Responsible for adjustments to the weather, port or starboard headsail (jib) sheet. They may often be heard shouting instructions to the 'grinders'.
8-12 Grinders Chosen largely for muscle-power, their job is to hoist the sails and adjust them as quickly as possible by tensioning the sheets using the 'coffee-grinder' winches.
13 Spinnaker Trimmer Has to think quickly and make rapid alterations to the set of the spinnaker. A key member of the crew.
14 Sewer/Halyard Man Packs the 'parachutes' in the pit below decks and feeds sails to the deckhands through the 'sewer' (forehatch). Mans the sail (-hoisting) halyards.
15 Foredeck Hand Helps the bowman position the massive spinnaker pole, liaises closely with the sewer man and helps hoist, stow and generally handle the sails.
16 Bowman The 'hero' who organises all the sail changes and acts as a forward lookout. In rough weather the bowman has the most difficult task and may be constantly under water.

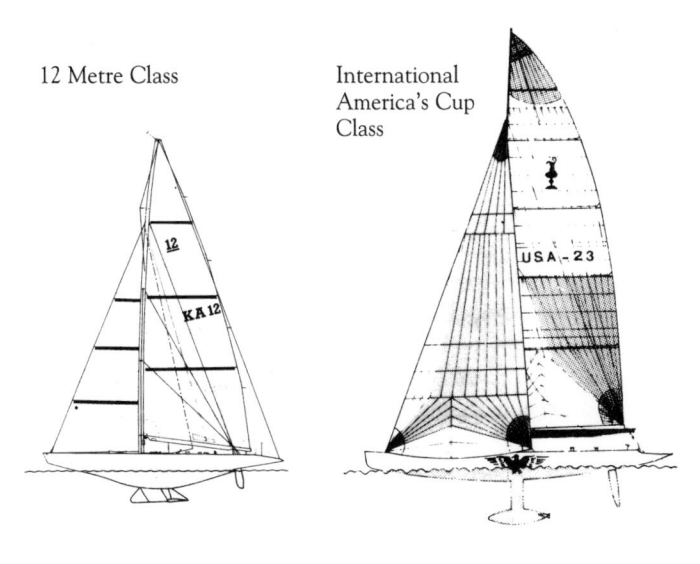

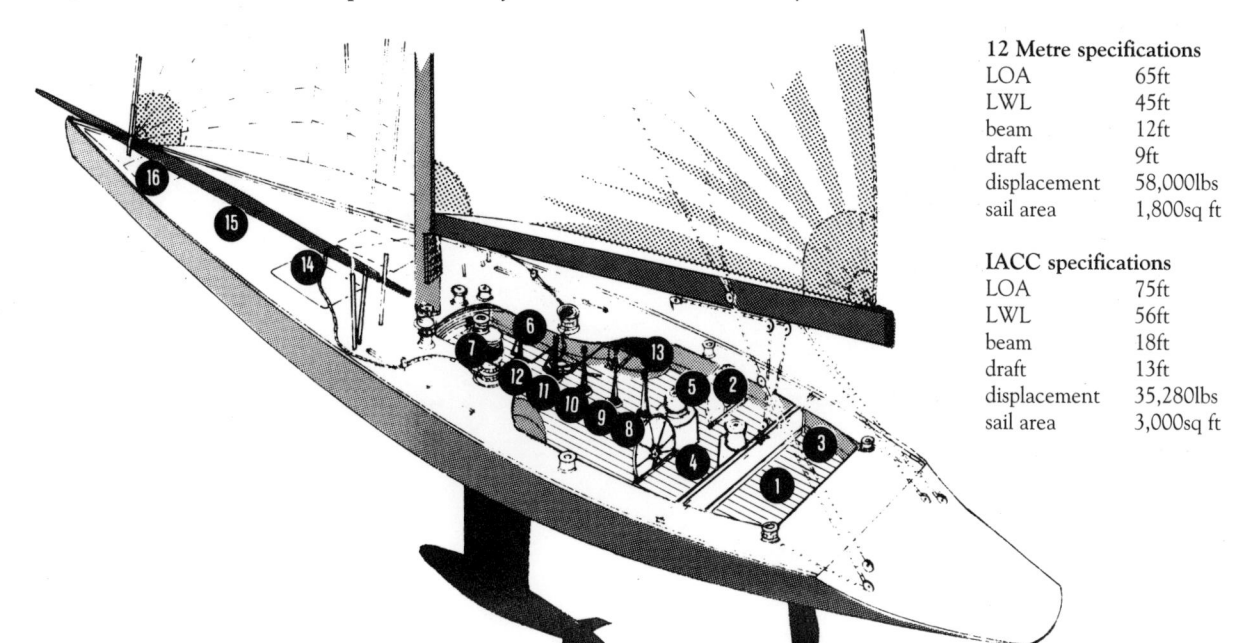

12 Metre specifications
LOA	65ft
LWL	45ft
beam	12ft
draft	9ft
displacement	58,000lbs
sail area	1,800sq ft

IACC specifications
LOA	75ft
LWL	56ft
beam	18ft
draft	13ft
displacement	35,280lbs
sail area	3,000sq ft

Research and Development

Since the international America's Cup Class first took the stage, designers have been striving for a breakthrough that would give their yachts enough edge on their competitors to ensure victory. However, such are the constraints of 'one designs' that many of the original features, particularly the keels, remain almost the same since the 12 Metre *Australia II* broke America's stranglehold on the Cup with her innovative winged appendage in 1983.

Much of current thinking has been about reducing weight on top while adding it to the keel below. Using the latest carbon fibre thread, intricately laid to give maximum strength, the hulls have been made progressively lighter, until many have become no more than man-made eggshells, immensely strong if force is applied from the most likely directions, but as weak as kittens if they should be struck 'below the belt' by a rogue wave. Thus the yachts have become progressively more highly tuned, leaving their unfortunate skippers to endure a frightening balancing act between triumph and disaster.

America's Cup Class hull shapes, like keels, leave little room for manoeuvre. Cutting off the yacht's nose may create advantages elsewhere, but waterline length, which is seldom sacrificed, remains the overriding principle in building a fast boat. However, the secrecy surrounding most competing yachts remains much the same as ever, and after hours of expensive tank testing, crews are still loathe to flaunt even the smallest design feature. The innovative 'Hula', or double skin, thought up by Team New Zealand in 2003, was one of them. It could have been a winner.

Sails are different. Not only are their secrets likely to be discovered early on, particularly their shape, but rapid advances in technology, largely fuelled by the America's Cup itself, may lead to many last minute changes. With the power of the yacht derived mainly from its sails, their design is crucial, and, although the practice of baking miles of kevlar and carbon thread between two layers of Myla film is becoming standard, there are many different ways of cutting them.

Soon after the 2007 match had been completed, Louis Vuitton withdrew their sponsorship. Team Alinghi, already preparing to defend the Cup again, declared that for the next series, to be held as early as 2009, there was to be a new, longer and faster America's Cup Class yacht. The design, which was to be some 90 ft with sliding or retractable keels, would not cause team Alinghi to lose any sleep, having had it in mind for some time. But for the challengers it was such a nightmare that Larry Ellison, who, as a master stroke, had signed Russell Coutts as his next skipper and helmsman, threatened to take fellow billionaire Ernesto Bertarelli to the American Supreme Court over the unfair protocol put forward by Bertarelli's chosen Challenger of Record the newly-formed Club Nautico Espanol de Vela and *Desafio Espanol*.

Already by 2007 the investment in the Cup by just four competing syndicates had exceeded the cost of NASA sending a space shuttle into orbit!

America's Cup Class yacht – Version 5

Length	24m
Beam	4m
Displacement	24tonnes
Upwind sails	350sq m
Downwind sails	700sq m
Mast height	33m

Mainsail At nearly 220 square metres, it is the yacht's most powerful sail, designed to generate lift like an aeroplane's wing. The sail may contain more than 65km of carbon fibre thread.

Genoa is made in the same way as the mainsail. America's Cup yachts will carry about six different sizes or 'codes' of genoas during a race.

Spinnaker and gennaker – enormous, colourful sails hoisted when a yacht is sailing downwind. The spinnaker is usually a 'symmetrical' sail, meaning that both sides are the same length, and may be as large as two tennis courts. A gennaker is about half the size of a spinnaker, used mostly in light airs.

Spinnaker Boom Hollow carbon fibre.

Rigging About 3,300ft (1000m) of stainless steel cable.

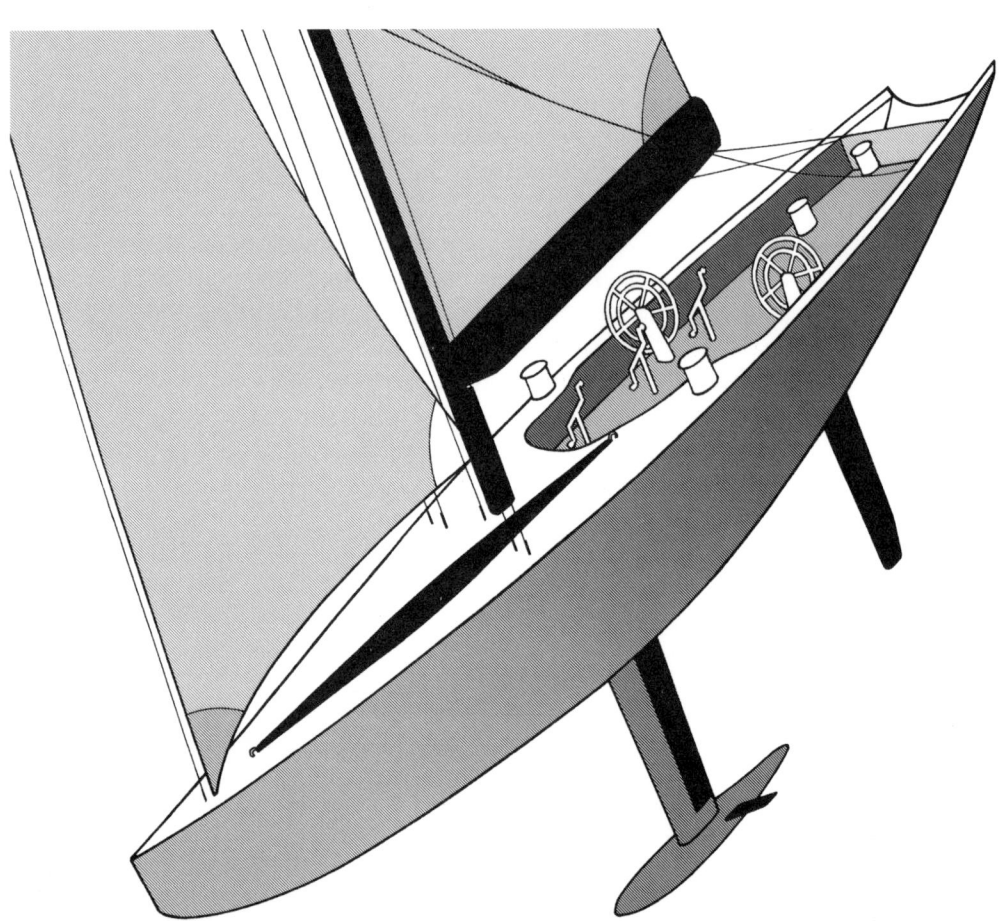

Boom Hollow carbon fibre, deep for strength.

Cutaway Stern

Steering Wheels The boat may be steered from either side.

Rudder A thin carbon fibre foil, which has to be strong enough to withstand heavy lateral pressure.

Coffee Grinders Geared, double sided handles so that two 'gorillas' may wind in the 'sheets'.

Winches Turned at different speeds by the 'coffee grinders'.

Trim Tab is constantly adjusted from the cockpit to enable the keel to perform to maximum advantage.

Deck Honeycomb construction like the hull. Ultra strong with carbon fibre skin.

Hull Just 2in thick. Of honeycomb construction with carbon fibre surfaces. About 79ft (24m) long, weighing 2 tonnes.

Keel Consists of an aerodynamic strut with a torpedo shaped ballast bulb with wings weighing about 19 tonnes, or 80% of the boat.

THE PAINTINGS

Picking out the more exciting incidents from each Cup series was much more difficult than I had first expected. Indeed, in some of the earlier matches, apart from plenty of wenching and hard drinking, at first sight nothing much of note seemed to have happened. Eventually it was the newspaper cuttings of the day that provided most of the answers, but not all.

One match that left me cold was that between *Atalanta* and *Mischief* in 1881. I looked everywhere for an engaging story, but no – *Atalanta* was a 'dog', and she could hardly have beaten a coal barge. Then, from a battered old ship's log, I discovered that her Canadian skipper had been as stubborn as his ship, and he had refused to go to the start of the second race until he and his crew had finished their breakfast. Breakfast in America is often served in the village stores, and we believe that when the race committee went looking for the errant crew, that is precisely where they fond them. It has made a great painting.

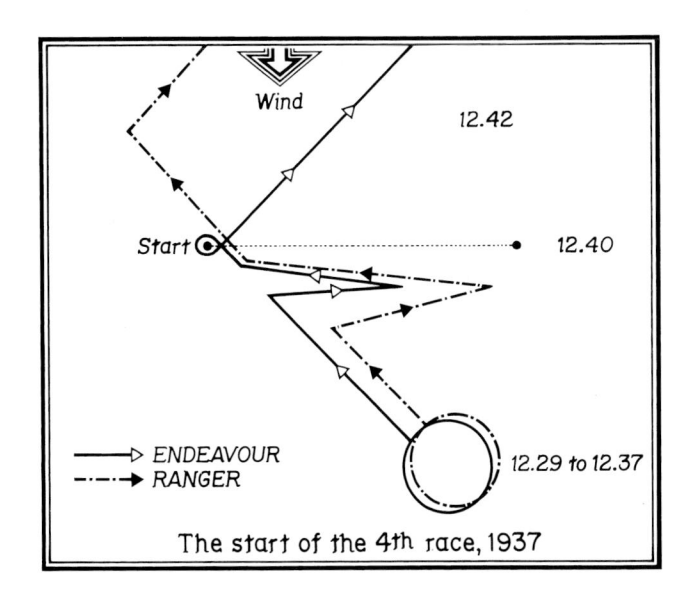

One better-known incident that needs explanation is that of *Ranger* forcing *Endeavour II* early over the line in 1937. This was painted with the help of photographs and a diagram, reproduced here, from Sir Fisher Dilke's book, *Observer on Ranger*. The painting may seem over-dramatised, but Vanderbilt said at the time that the two boats would have touched 'if *Endeavour* had not been travelling faster than the *Ranger*'.

Throughout, we have tried to mix drama with tranquillity, and to ring the changes between light and shade, and sea, sky and wind conditions, in order to give the widely differing scenes additional merit. We believe that these were the actual conditions prevailing on each occasion and that they agree with the often misinterpreted accounts of the time. It is also interesting to compare the paintings of the earlier boats with those of the 12 Metres, and it will be seen that the artist has achieved a subtle transition between ancient and modern, and between 'old' seas and 'new' seas.

The rare luminosity of Tim Thompson's work is primarily the result of a painstaking technique practised by the Van de Veldes and later by the nineteenth-century masters of marine art. Applying layers of thin translucent washes, Tim carefully blends the colours with deft strokes from one of a fistful of fan brushes, and the details, such as the ropes and the sail stitching, is laid on so cleverly that it is hard to find a break in the smooth finished surface of the canvas.

For me it has been an inspiration working with him, and I hope that the following reproductions of the America's Cup Collection will give equal pleasure to all those who see them.

1851
AMERICA defeats the BRITISH FLEET

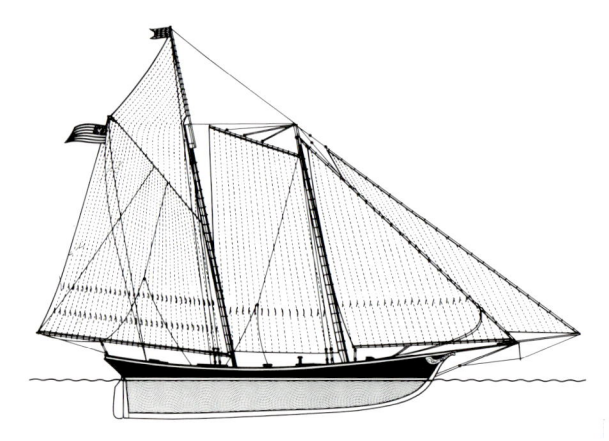

America	LOA: 101ft	Owner:
New York	LWL: 90ft	John Stevens and
Yacht Club	beam: 23ft	syndicate
	draft: 11ft	Designer:
	displacement: 170.55 tons	George Steers
	sail area: 5263sq ft	Builder:
		William Brown
		Skipper:
		Chas. Brown

During the mid-nineteenth century the American clipper ships and pilot boats were probably the most seaworthy and speedy craft in the world. By 1851, the year of the first World's Fair, a great international exposition to be held in London, American boat builders had become famous among seamen of every nation. Encouraged by the promoters of the Fair, some New York businessmen therefore persuaded John C. Stevens, Commodore of the recently formed New York Yacht Club, to commission a yacht to compete against the British for money. She was to be named *America*.

The Commodore had a talk with his friends Hamilton Weeks, George L. Schuyler, James Hamilton and J. B. Finlay and they decided to ask George Steers, the son of a Devonshire shipwright, who had designed many successful pilot boats, to draw them a fast schooner of about 90ft (30m). William Brown, whose yard was chosen to build her, became so enthralled with the project that he offered to complete *America* for £30,000 ($45,000) to be paid out of his own pocket if she failed to beat all opposition. The syndicate agreed that such an offer should not be declined.

America sailed from New York early in June 1851, bound for Le Havre. As the crew battened down for the open sea, 'Old Dick Brown', a *Sandy Hook* pilot, who had been entrusted with the command of the little boat, thundered: 'If there be a white-livered dog among you who wants to step ashore, now is the time to yelp.' Not a man yelped but one of the nine crew climbed up on a hatch and raising his cap called for three cheers for the ship and skipper Brown. The passage took them twenty-one days; it was, in fact, the first time that a yacht had crossed the Atlantic in either direction.

Commodore Stevens joined her in France, where, with help from her designer George Steers, she was prepared immediately for battle with a racing rig. As soon as she was ready she sailed for Cowes on the Isle of Wight, which was then, as it is now, the yachting headquarters of Great Britain.

Commodore Stevens had a sack of gold coins in his cabin and because it was his intention to wager enough money to more than recover the cost of the boat, he was determined not to show his hand too soon. But his plans were to come to naught.

Forced to wait for daylight six miles from Cowes, *America* was met by the cutter *Laverock*, a very fast yacht, which had courteously arrived to escort her and incidentally get a feel for her performance. It would have been the easiest thing in the world to have let *Laverock* beat *America* to the shore, but the blood was already running too hot in the Commodore's veins. In no way could he resist a contest, and the British yacht was thrashed soundly.

The British did not know what to make of *America*. *The Times* reported: 'She has a low black hull, and two noble sticks of extreme rake without an extra rope. When close to her you see that her stem is as sharp as a knife blade, scooped away until she swells again towards the stern.' The absence of a jib boom and a fore topmast surprised the opposition, and although it was the custom in England to cut baggy sails to hold the wind, the *America*'s sails were as flat as boards.

The news that the Yankee schooner was fast spread like wildfire and Stevens was unable to lay a single wager. The only prize that the Royal Yacht Squadron were prepared to put up was a cup valued at 100 guineas (about $180), which was to be awarded to the winner of an international regatta to be held on 22 August as part of the celebrations for the World's Fair.

On the morning of the race, more spectator craft gathered off Cowes than had even been seen together in the history of yachting. The preparatory signal was fired at 09.55 from the Squadron battery and most of the fifteen competitors, anchored in a double line, got under way smartly, although *America* seemed in no mood to hurry. At 10.00 the starting gun boomed out and the fleet sailed away to the east with *America* scything through the opposition until she was lying in fifth position.

'Old Dick Brown', at the helm of *America*, was by now being so severely jostled that he decided to break away and pass inside the *Nab* light vessel which marked the eastern end of the course. The wind was blowing up from the south–south–west and there is no doubt that the manoeuvre gave him a considerable advantage over the leading boats standing off to pass round the *Nab*.

Followed by the remainder of the British fleet, *America*, now with a 'bone in her teeth', romped towards St Catherine's Point, losing her flying jib on the way. Although two yachts, *Freak* and *Volante*, made up some ground tacking close under the cliffs, they unfortunately collided, and when shortly afterwards *Arrow* went aground, with *Alarm* standing by to give assistance, *America* was out on her own. She reached the Needles at 17.30 some eight miles ahead of *Aurora*, and when she met and saluted the Royal Yacht *Victoria and Albert*, she was the only boat in sight.

The following morning the owner of *Brilliant*, the fifth boat to finish, formally protested that *America* had passed the wrong side of the *Nab* light vessel and should be disqualified. But this was promptly overruled by the Earl of Wilton, Commodore of the Royal Yacht Squadron, who explained diplomatically that an observer from the Squadron and a local pilot had sailed on board *America* and that by mistake she had been given two different sets of racing instructions.

Some were suspicious that *America* had won because of a secret propeller, but other more aspiring yachtsmen examined her advanced design. One, the Marquis of Anglesey, said after long deliberation: 'I've learned one thing. I've been sailing my yacht stern first for the last twenty years!'

As America *passes inside the* Nab *light vessel, pushing against the tide, her afterguard watch as* Arrow, Bacchante *(hidden),* Constance *and* Gypsy Queen *conform to 'the other set of rules'. The* Volante, *followed by* Aurora *and the remainder of the fleet, alters course and gives chase*

America's afterguard left to right: Capt Brown, Col Hamilton, observer RYS, Commodore Stevens, pilot, crew member

Volante Aurora Constance Bacchante America (Hidden, Gypsy Queen) Arrow Nab light vessel

1870 MAGIC defeats CAMBRIA

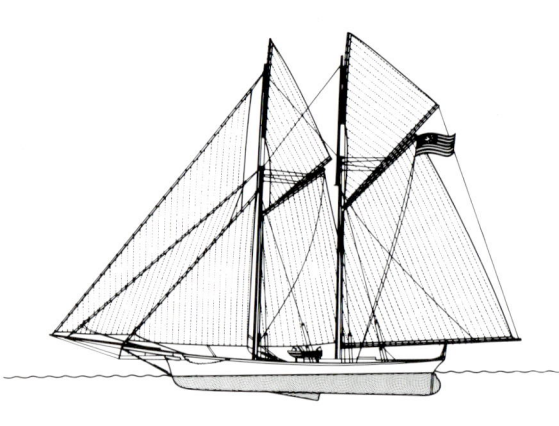

Magic	LOA: 84ft	Owner:
New York	LWL: 79ft	Franklin Osgood
Yacht Club	beam: 20ft 9in	Designer:
	draft: 6ft 3in	R. F. Loper
	draft with board: 17ft	Builder:
	displacement: 112.2 tons	T. Byerly & Son
	sail area: 1680sq ft	Skipper:
	(lowers only)	Andrew Comstock

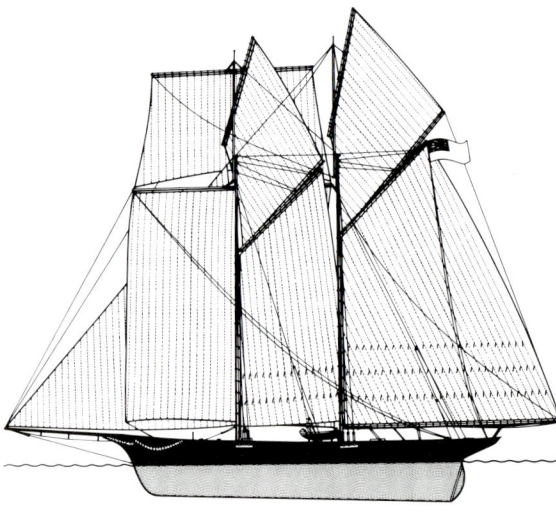

Cambria	LOA: 108ft	Owner:
Royal	LWL: 98ft	James Ashbury
Thames	beam: 21ft	Designer:
	draft: 12ft	Michael Ratsey
	displacement: 228 tons	Builder:
	sail area: 8602sq ft	Michael Ratsey
		Skipper:
		J. Tannock

After the *America*'s heroic win in 1851, her syndicate sold her in England to Lord de Blaquiere, but they continued showing off the Cup in their respective homes until in 1857 George Schuyler had the bright idea of saving on the silver polish by presenting it to the New York Yacht Club as an international yachting trophy. In a letter sent to the Club, later known as the first Deed of Gift, the syndicate made certain stipulations, concluding: 'It is to be distinctly understood that the Cup is to be the property of the Club, and not of the members thereof, or owners of the vessels winning it in a match; and that the condition of keeping it open to be sailed for by yacht clubs of all foreign countries, upon the terms above laid down, shall forever attach to it, thus making it perpetually a Challenge Cup for friendly competition between foreign countries.' But, as it happened, the Yankees were given twelve more years to crow about their victory and when battle recommenced there was nothing friendly about it at all.

British yachtsmen had misguidedly been in no hurry to take up the challenge, for in America there had been a rapid decline in yachting due to the Civil War. During this period several boats, following the *America*'s example, sailed in English waters, including *Fleetwing, Henrietta* and *Vesta*, which raced across the Atlantic for the first time in history. The race, won by *Henrietta* in just under fourteen days, was unfortunately marred by tragedy when six men were swept off *Fleetwing* by a giant wave, and generally the expedition was to have little success. More significant, however, was the arrival in 1868 of the large American schooner *Sappho*, sent across by her owners to be sold. Although she had acquitted herself well in the United States, they gave strict instructions that she was not to be tested but, as had happened in 1851, her skipper could not resist the temptation, and in a race held once again around the Isle of Wight she was soundly beaten by four British yachts including Mr James Ashbury's *Cambria*, which won.

It was this that no doubt encouraged Ashbury, a man who had made a fortune on the railways, to write to the New York Yacht Club during 1869 initiating the first challenge for the America's Cup.

The tedious correspondence which followed became almost acrimonious at times, and the details were debated to such lengths that no match could be arranged until the following season. Among his many requirements Ashbury insisted that, per the rules of the Royal Yacht Squadron, centreboarders should not be eligible to compete, but the New York Yacht Club, turning a deaf ear, countered that his own challenge was unacceptable as it had not come through a recognised yacht club, and Ashbury was thus forced to challenge instead through the Royal Thames. Another of Ashbury's proposals had been that he should race against their boat across the Atlantic and then around Long Island, but although the committee agreed to the first part, the second idea was never settled, and when the *Cambria* subsequently defeated the American schooner *Dauntless* on their passage to New York, it became clear why no decision had been reached. The New York Yacht Club had no intention of handing over the Cup on a plate, and when they argued that the terms should be similar to those of the first match, Ashbury realised that the New York Yacht Club were intending to knock him out with all the guns that they could bring to bear.

That the *Cambria* should now be asked to take on the Club's entire fleet seemed not a little unsporting, and to many it was a gross misinterpretation of the Deed of Gift. It was one thing for a yacht like the *America* to join in and win a friendly club race, but quite another for a yacht to be taken on by a well-prepared and hostile armada, intent only on preventing the Cup leaving the country. The Deed definitely talked about a match, not a war, and although it could have been said that *America* had been jostled by a number of British competitors in 1851, nothing quite compared with the treatment planned for the gallant *Cambria* in 1870!

The New York Yacht Club had invited Ashbury to sail a single race over a course starting off Staten Island and thence through the narrows and round the *Sandy Hook* lightship, a distance of about 36 nautical miles. The morning of 8 August, the day set for the race, broke with leaden skies, and when *Cambria* and her eighteen opponents took up their stations the challenger was generously given the weather end of the line. According to the custom of the day the start was from anchor, all the yachts being drawn up with their chains short and their sails down, and as the signal was given there was feverish activity as the crews sweated at the windlasses and struggled with the halyards to hoist the sails.

The best position was, as it happened, of no benefit to *Cambria*, for as the sun broke through the wind shifted from the south–west to the south–east, making her the most leewardly boat of the fleet. Among the large number of spectator craft gathered to witness the inaugural defence of the America's Cup stood out a tug bedecked with British colours, and as *Cambria* got under way the tug's brass band blared out 'Rule Britannia', but all to no avail. She had a poor start and was immediately besieged by most of the boats around her.

The little centreboard schooner *Magic* was the first away, and with the advantage of her shallower draft she was able to stand over towards the shore and establish a convincing lead, but by the Spit Buoy the old *America*, which had been hastily fitted out by the Navy Department to defend her title, had almost caught her up. It was soon after this that *Cambria*, who was already nineteen minutes behind, was struck by another boat, losing a port shroud and her fore topmast-backstay, the *Spirit of the Times* subsequently reporting, 'she suffered a little delay by being fouled by *Tarolinta*, which, being on the starboard tack should have kept away'. *Magic* went on to win, but *Cambria*, probably as a result of this collision, lost her fore topmast as she gybed for the run home, and could not manage better than tenth place, finishing some fourteen minutes behind *America*.

Thus the first attempt to lift the Cup had failed but, undaunted, Ashbury continued racing for a time in America. Finally, at last confident that the New York Yacht Club would ease the rules, he took his boat home and sold her as a trading vessel, *Cambria* later making money for her owners on the west coast of Africa in the humbler occupation to which fate had condemned her.

As Magic, pursued by the America, makes for the Sandy Hook lightship, Cambria is fouled by the Tarolinta, which carries away part of her rigging while going about

broken shroud

Sandy Hook lightship   *Fleetwing*   marker flag   *Magic*   America (half hidden)   *Cambria*   *Tarolinta*   *Dauntless*   *Idler*   *Phantom*

1871
COLUMBIA and SAPPHO
defeat LIVONIA

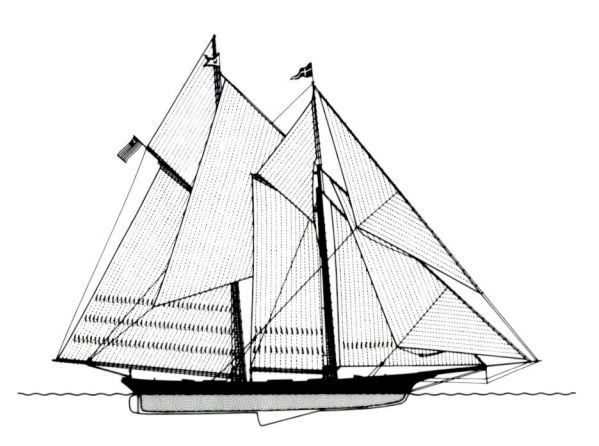

Columbia
New York
Yacht Club
LOA: 107ft 10in
LWL: 96ft 5in
beam: 25ft 6in
draft: 5ft 11in
draft with board: 22ft
displacement: 220 tons
sail area: not known
Owner:
Franklin Osgood
Designer:
J. B. van Deusen
Builder:
J. B. van Deusen
Skipper:
Nelson Comstock

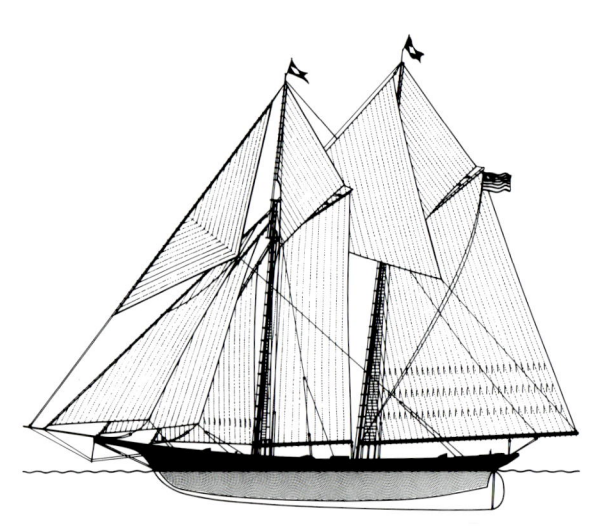

Sappho
New York
Yacht Club
LOA: 135ft
LWL: 119ft 4in
beam: 27ft 4in
draft: 12ft 8in
displacement: 310 tons
sail area: 9060sq ft
Owner:
Col. W. P. Douglas
Designer:
C. & R. Poillon
Builder:
C. & R. Poillon
Skipper:
Sam Greenwood

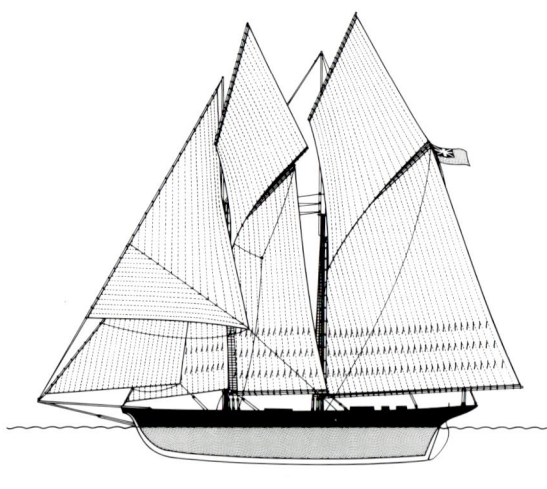

Livonia
Royal
Harwich
LOA: 127ft
LWL: 106ft 6in
beam: 23ft 7in
draft: 12ft 6in
displacement: 280 tons
sail area: 18,153sq ft
Owner:
James Ashbury
Designer:
Michael Ratsey
Builder:
Michael Ratsey
Skipper:
J. R. Woods

Directly after his arrival in England, following the defeat of his schooner *Cambria* in the first challenge for the America's Cup, James Ashbury asked Michael Ratsey of Cowes to build him a new yacht expressly to win the Cup in 1871. This second challenge caused even greater controversy than in 1870, although it resulted in certain concessions being granted by the New York Yacht Club.

No money was spared on *Livonia* and she was constructed of oak and teak to combine all that was best in English and American design. But so confident were the Americans in their choice from existing yachts that no new vessels were put on the stocks. However, in his correspondence with the New York Yacht Club before setting out, Ashbury had insisted upon his right to appear as the representative of no less than twelve yacht clubs, with the opportunity to sail twelve races on twelve different days. If he managed to win any one of these races the club he was representing on that day was to be awarded the Cup! The Club held a meeting to consider Ashbury's proposals, but although they decided that he could represent only the Royal Harwich Yacht Club, they also conceded that he should not be put against the whole of their fleet, as in 1870!

The *Livonia* sailed for America before the final details had been arranged and Ashbury continued to argue his case in New York until it was settled that he was to sail the best of seven races against any one of four defenders.

On the day of the opening race there were as many spectators present as there had been the year before. Two keel schooners, *Dauntless* and *Sappho*, and two centreboard schooners, *Palmer* and *Columbia*, had been selected to defend the Cup, but *Columbia* was the first to establish her superiority over the British boat. Gaining three minutes before the Narrows she never gave *Livonia* a ghost of a chance and won by a wide margin.

The next race was to take place on 18 October 1871 from the Sandy Hook lightship 20 miles to windward and return, but on the day a course four points from the wind was the best that the committee could achieve, and by failing to issue clear racing instructions they created a situation not unlike that favouring *America* in 1851. In a blustery north-westerly, *Livonia* reached the outer mark ahead of *Columbia*, who had again been chosen to represent the New York Club, but because her skipper had not been told from which side to round it, he left the mark boat to starboard, as was then the rule in England.

This decision cost *Livonia* the race. Compelled to gybe because of the wind direction, her sails crashed over with the brute force of a charging elephant, and she was left in such disarray that her crew, including a wretched man stationed aloft to kick over the topsail, took several moments to recover and sharpen up. Quick to take advantage, Mr Osgood on board *Columbia*, steered his vessel between the staggering *Livonia* and the mark, tacked around it smartly and, stowing his topsails in the strengthening gale, took her speeding home to win comfortably on a reach.

It was apparent that Osgood had asked the committee about rounding the mark, and when Ashbury protested that *Columbia* had contravened sailing instructions, he was told that: 'The sailing regulations for the outside course leave the manner of turning the stake-boat optional.' Ashbury was furious.

Although *Dauntless* was chosen as defender in the third race, she was disabled while under tow, and because the *Sappho* and the *Palmer* were not on hand, *Columbia*, without her captain who had been injured, was again called to the line. But, expecting a rest day, her crew had been indulging a little too freely and before long *Columbia*'s flying jib carried away and her steering gear broke. *Livonia* romped home over fifteen minutes ahead to win the only race of any series to be taken by a challenger until 1920.

The win was not a popular one, and the fourth race was witnessed by only a solitary spectator craft! *Sappho*, then the largest yacht ever built in America, won easily as she did again in the fifth and final race. But Ashbury did not take his defeat lightly. Claiming the sixth and seventh races, when he had gone to the line but there had been no boat to meet him, the second race won on protest, and the third taken fairly by a distance, he declared that he had won four out of seven contests and the Cup was his!

The committee took no heed of his claims, beyond acknowledging his letter, but when he continued to attack them after his return to England, they sent back all the cups he had presented to their club.

So ended one of the unhappier moments in the Cup's history. It was said that Ashbury later smoked a pipe of peace with the New York Yacht Club when he entered for a regatta at Le Havre the following season, but the owner of *Sappho*, who was there, declined to race him.

Columbia tacks round the stake-boat as the crew on the staggering *Livonia*, which has gybed from the other side, struggle to control her

man on topsail

Livonia   *Columbia*   stake-boat

1876
MADELEINE defeats COUNTESS OF DUFFERIN

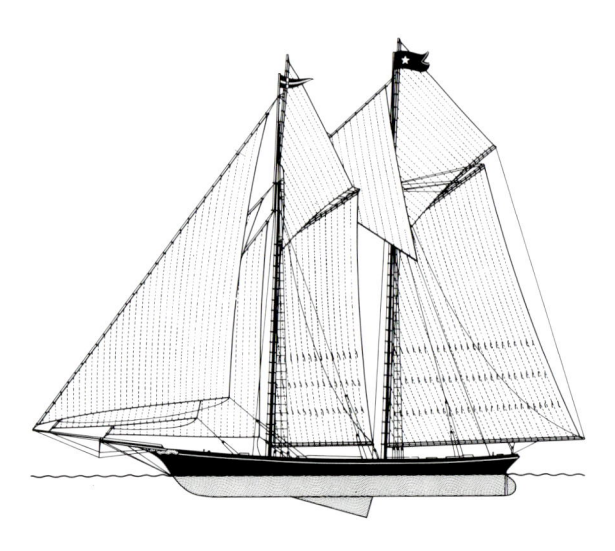

Madeleine	LOA: 106ft 4in	Owner:
New York	LWL: 95ft	John S. Dickerson
Yacht Club	beam: 24ft 3in	Designer:
	draft: 7ft 3in	David Kirby
	draft with board: 19ft 6in	Builder:
	displacement: 152 tons	David Kirby
	sail area: 17,231sq ft	Skipper:
		Josephus Williams

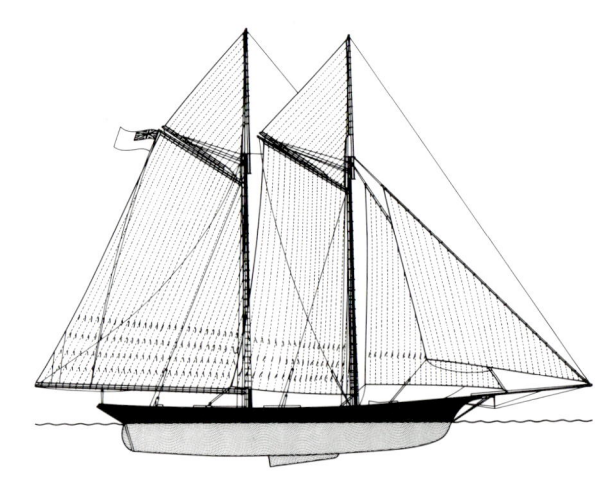

Countess of	LOA: 107ft	Owner:
Dufferin	LWL: 74ft 7in	Major Charles Gifford
Royal	beam: 24ft	and syndicate
Canadian	draft: 6ft 6in	Designer
	draft with board: 18ft	Alexander Cuthbert
	displacement: 138 tons	Builder:
	sail area: not known	Alexander Cuthbert
		Skipper:
		J. E. Ellsworth

Interest in yacht racing had increased greatly as a result of the first two challenges for the America's Cup; but although it was felt that Ashbury's claim to the Cup was ludicrous, at the same time many believed that he had been unfairly treated in America and it was a waste of time and money to take a yacht over there again. It was therefore hardly surprising that no new British challenger materialised, and that it was left to others to try their hands.

Five years passed before Major Charles Gifford, Vice-Commodore of the Royal Canadian Yacht Club, formed a syndicate and submitted a challenge for the already famous trophy, and when he asked for the six months' notice to be waived, the New York Yacht Club, in generous mood, not only assented but also offered him the opportunity of three deciding races instead of one. Where Ashbury had failed, Gifford, determined to succeed, had asked for one further concession, and when this was omitted from the Club's reply, he wrote to them again complaining of their unfair advantage with so many yachts to choose from, and suggesting that in future they should agree to nominate just one. Amazingly, and by eleven votes to five, they did.

Gifford's entry, the 107ft (32.6m) *Countess of Dufferin*, had been 'specially designed' for the occasion by Captain Alexander Cuthbert, a not very imaginative fellow, who had almost certainly 'stolen' her lines from a New Jersey boatbuilder. But although he felt that she had an excellent chance of winning, and the Dominion newspapers were full of flattery, the Americans thought otherwise. Commanded by Gifford, but sailed by Cuthbert, the *Countess* set out from Ontario via Quebec early in June, and having negotiated the St Lawrence river she skirted the coast of Nova Scotia arriving in New York, after an uneventful passage, in mid July.

The press immediately had a field day. 'There is nothing foreign about her', quoted one leading journalist. 'Her shape is American, her rig is American, her blocks are the Waterman patent of New York. Her steering gear is of New York manufacture, and from stem to stern, inside and out, alow and aloft, she is simply a Yankee boat built in Canada.' Perhaps that would have passed if others had not described her hull 'as rough as a nutmeg scraper', and her sails 'like a purser's shirt on a handspike'. Indeed to critical eyes the *Countess*'s many defects were more reminiscent of a clumsy coaster than of a racing schooner intent on snatching the America's Cup, and it was in this atmosphere that the New York Yacht Club set about choosing a defender from the large number of vessels believed capable of beating her.

There were already five yachts on the New York Yacht Club shortlist, *Columbia, Palmer, Tidal Wave, Idler* and *Madeleine*, but on the day of the first-ever American elimination race only *Madeleine* and *Idler* showed up. *Madeleine* won convincingly and the committee had no hesitation in selecting her to defend the Cup.

In contrast to the *Countess of Dufferin*, which she equalled in size, the schooner *Madeleine*, owned by John S. Dickerson, Commodore of the Brooklyn Yacht Club, had been splendidly prepared and expertly manned. Built as a sloop eight years earlier in 1868, she had since undergone extensive alterations, and from 1873, when she was said to have won every race in which she started, she had built up a formidable reputation.

Madeleine's first opportunity to get the measure of her opponent came in the Brenton Reef race, when the *Countess*, having sportingly taken on four other schooners over a long ocean course, finished so far behind that it was thought she had foundered. Her performance was so bad that Gifford asked for the Cup races to be postponed so that he could get some new sails cut and generally get her smartened up. The New York *Spirit of the Times* later reported: 'Her owner had not been here many days before he saw that his yacht was a monstrosity. He at once called to his aid all the yachting skill which New York possessed, and completely transformed his yacht: booms were lengthened out, clouds of canvas were fitted, a full crew of the choicest Yankee tars were selected, and the best sailing master in New York was engaged.' In truth the Americans and the New York Yacht Club had been more than helpful, but was it enough?

It had finally been arranged to hold the first race over the New York Yacht Club inside course of 11 August. *Madeleine* had been towed down from Greenwich, Connecticut, where her copper bottom had been treated with oil and tallow to make her slide easily through the water, and the *Countess*, which had been hauled out at Port Richmond, had also had her bottom potleaded and generally given a thorough manicure.

It was to be the first occasion on which the start was under canvas, and as the two contenders crossed the line and beat southwards into the moderate breeze, the audience on the twelve excursion steamers and about twenty yachts, including the old *America*, were treated to a grand spectacle.

Although *Madeleine* was not slow to show her paces, it was commendable that the *Countess* kept her in sight, and when the Yankee schooner, partly because of the heavy swell, overstood the lightship, *Countess* did by far the better turn, passing it only five minutes behind. But she never made up the deficit, and having lost the second race to *Madeleine* by more than twenty-seven minutes, and by nineteen minutes to the twenty-five-year-old veteran, *America*, which on this occasion was timed, though of course *hors concours*, everyone agreed that enough was enough!

Madeleine rounds the *Sandy Hook* lightship, and as her crew struggle to set more sail, the *Countess of Dufferin* followed by the old *America*, which is only out for the ride, looms up behind

changing sails

Countess of Dufferin   Sandy Hook lightship   America   Madeleine   steam yacht

1881 MISCHIEF defeats ATALANTA

Mischief	LOA: 67ft 5in	Owner:
New York	LWL: 61ft	Joseph Busk
Yacht Club	beam: 19ft 10in	Designer:
	draft: 5ft 6in	A. Cary Smith
	draft with board: 16ft	Builder:
	displacement: 79 tons	Harlan and Hollingsworth
	sail area: not known	Skipper:
		Nathaniel Clock

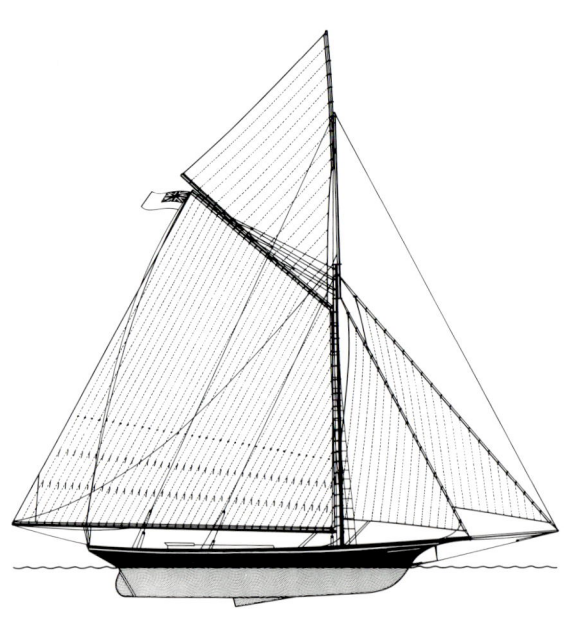

Atalanta	LOA: 70ft	Owner:
Bay of	LWL: 64ft	Alexander Cuthbert
Quinte	beam: 19ft	Designer:
(Canada)	draft: 5ft 6in	Alexander Cuthbert
	draft with board: 16ft 6in	Builder:
	displacement: 84 tons	Alexander Cuthbert
	sail area: not known	Skipper:
		Alexander Cuthbert

The second Canadian challenge was not received until well into 1881, when the Secretary of the tiny Bay of Quinte Yacht Club of Belleville, Ontario was asked by a syndicate, headed by Mr Albert Cuthbert, to submit a challenge requesting that 'in consequence of the season being so far advanced, the six months' notice be waived'. It seemed that late challenges were becoming a habit. Or was it perhaps that the challengers were trying to catch the New York Yacht Club off guard, without suitable boats for the Cup? In the event the NYYC accepted, for judging by the unimpressive first Canadian challenge, it did not really seem to matter.

Not all Americans thought the same way, however, and for the first time in the Cup's history a yacht, *Pocahontas*, was built especially for the defence. It was also the first occasion that it was considered necessary to hold trial races, and after the wretched *Pocahontas* had been sent packing it was left to *Mischief* to narrowly gain selection from *Gracie* and *Hildegarde*. The days of the great schooners were already numbered, so 1881 also heralded the first Cup match between single-stickers, and yet another first was scored by *Mischief*, which was the first metal boat ever to defend the Cup, and only the second such yacht to have been built in America.

Most of the summer had gone by before the challenger took to the water. She was constructed of wood and designed by Cuthbert himself, who had also been responsible for the *Countess of Dufferin*. Instead of being sailed to New York by the ocean route, she was towed from the Great Lakes, at times by mule, through the Erie Canal. On occasions, when she proved too wide for the lock gates, her ballast had to be shifted to one side, and by the time she arrived down the Hudson River it was 30 October, and long after the yachting season had closed.

Cuthbert had named his new boat *Atalanta* after the daughter of a mythical Greek king, who had promised to marry any man who could sprint faster than herself but to have put to death all those who tried and failed. Judging, however, from her finish, described by one journalist as 'rough as a hedge fence', and her badly fitting suit of sails, it appeared unlikely, right from the outset, that Yankee heads would roll, and even more doubtful that any of them would be prepared to fall in love with her!

Mischief, although often referred to as 'The Iron Pot', was a prettier and better finished boat altogether, and she was considered to be one of the most competitive yachts in the world. Owned surprisingly by an Englishman, Captain Busk, she had much greater depth than other American yachts of that period and, aided by a centreboard let down through her keel, she was considerably more stable. It was just as well, for by the time that the races were eventually held the weather had broken completely, and the series was only noted for its fog, lashing rain and high winds.

The first of the best of three races was delayed until 9 November when, watched by only a handful of spectators, the two yachts ploughed off up the inside course, closely followed by *Gracie*, which had been given permission to go along for the ride. The largely amateur crew of inshore Canadians, who had alone taken a reef in their mainsail, were quickly overhauled by both American boats, and ultimately they were left so far astern that the committee did not even bother to wait for them!

As a result, so little interest was shown in the second race that only a solitary sidewheeler was in attendance, and she soon went home. But although this too was a disaster for the Canadians, who lost their spinnaker pole and finished over forty minutes behind both *Mischief* and *Gracie*, it was to be remembered by the committee for other reasons.

After two days of dirty weather, the morning had dawned magnificently, with a fresh breeze blowing from the north-west. At 8am the tug *Luckenbach*, having picked up the race committee from pier No 3 on the East River, had made for Staten Island where they were to rendezvous with the two contestants and tow them immediately to the start. *Mischief*, waiting off Tompkinsville, secured her line, but when it was found that *Atalanta* was not ready, she cast off again and made her own way out to sea. It was almost an hour later when Captain Cuthbert and his merry crew appeared at last on the jetty, and the committee were not a little upset on discovering that the Canadians had only just been taking a very leisurely breakfast!

The *Spirit of the Times* summed up the result as follows: 'The *Mischief* distanced the *Atalanta*, a new yacht, hastily built, totally untried, and miserably equipped with misfitting sails, which was bungled round the course by an alleged crew, who would have been over-matched in trying to handle a canal-boat in a fog – only this, and nothing more.'

When Cuthbert, undaunted by his drubbing, declared his intention to challenge for a third time the following season, the New York Yacht Club had no alternative but to change the rules by banning all clubs without an ocean regatta course from ever competing again.

The tug Luckenbach *stands by as members of the committee look for the crew of* Atalanta. Mischief *meanwhile puts to sea and* Gracie, *riding the flood-tide like a racehorse, makes for the distant starting line committee enter Tompkinsville Stores*

Gracie   *Luckenbach* (committee tug)   *Atalanta*   Mischief

1885 PURITAN defeats GENESTA

Puritan
New York Yacht Club

LOA: 94ft
LWL: 81ft 1in
beam: 22ft 7in
draft: 8ft 8in
draft with board: 20ft
displacement: 140 tons
sail area: 7982sq ft

Owner:
J. Malcolm Forbes and General Charles J. Paine and syndicate
Designer:
Edward Burgess
Builder:
George Lawley & Son
Skipper:
Aubrey J. Crocker

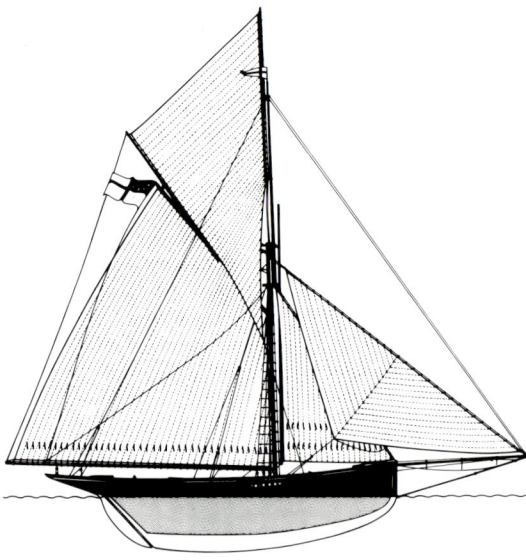

Genesta
Royal Yacht Squadron

LOA: 96ft 5in
LWL: 81ft 7in
beam: 15ft
draft: 13ft 6in
displacement: 80 tons
sail area: 7150sq ft

Owner:
Sir Richard Sutton
Designer:
J. Beavor-Webb
Builder:
D. & W. Henderson
Skipper:
John Carter

In February 1885 an official challenge was received by the New York Yacht Club from the British Designer J. Beavor-Webb on behalf of the Royal Yacht Squadron and Sir Richard Sutton, owner of the cutter *Genesta*. Previously Beavor-Webb had written to the Secretary of the Club suggesting that owners of two of the boats he had designed would like to challenge for the Cup and it had been agreed that if *Genesta* was defeated, *Galatea*, owned by Lieutenant William Henn, RN, would race for the America's Cup the following year.

In 1882 George L. Schuyler, the only surviving member of the first America's Cup syndicate, had been asked to draw up 'the second Deed of Gift', amending the rules to ensure that the America's Cup continued not only as a test of speed but also one of endurance. The 1881 challenger, *Atalanta*, had been towed to New York all the way from Canada, and this was no longer considered 'cricket', nor were challengers to be allowed to arrive as deck cargo on the increasing number of steamers capable of carrying them. The new rules, circulated to all foreign yacht clubs, stated that in future only large sea-going yachts, which had arrived under sail on their own bottoms, would be acceptable, and the New York Yacht Club would require six months' notice from any challenger in order to give them time to choose a suitable opponent.

The British cutter made her first appearance in May 1884, when she defeated all opposition at the New Thames Yacht Club regatta. Because of her deep, narrow hull and tapered stern *Genesta* was described by the press as 'an exceptionally attractive yacht with slim lines, likely to be a slippery customer', and before long news of her successes was being cabled across the Atlantic.

The American yachts, known as 'skimming dishes' at that time, were as different from the British 'planks on edges' as the *America* had been from the British boats in 1851, and the two sloops built to defend the Cup were both beamy and shallow. Instead of the deep keel favoured by British designers, the yachts were fitted, for the first time, with a combination of leaded keel and the traditional American centreboard. They were named *Priscilla* and *Puritan*. Selection trials were sailed during the summer of 1885, resulting in *Puritan* being chosen to represent America in the coming contest. She had a mast of Oregon pine and a bowsprit, not unlike that of *Genesta*, 38ft (12m) long.

When *Genesta* arrived in American waters she was watched with interest, but her skipper, Captain Carter, carefully avoided any brushes with the opposition. Before the first race, which was to be held on the inshore course south of New York, *Genesta* was hauled out and her copper bottom was burnished to a mirror finish.

The first race had to be postponed because of lack of wind, but it was held on the following day, 8 September. The clear cloudless sky, and the promise of magnificent weather for the race, drew a large fleet of spectator craft to the start off the *Scotland* lightship, and they were soon to be rewarded by witnessing one of the more chivalrous events in the Cup's history.

Both yachts, as they waited for the starting whistle, made for the line on different tacks. *Genesta*, moving fast on the starboard tack, had right of way, and when she was crossed by *Puritan*, whose skipper, either miscalculating or intending to bluff, shaved her bow, Captain Carter quite correctly held his course. Although *Puritan*'s skipper tried to luff, he had no chance, and running from the helm as *Genesta*'s long bowsprit ripped through the clew of his mainsail, he was lucky to escape with his life. The leech rope on *Puritan*, however, failed to part, snapping off *Genesta*'s bowsprit at the gammon like a rotten carrot and leaving her out of action.

Sir Richard Sutton hailed the committee boat, which quickly steamed towards *Genesta*, and asked how much time he had for lodging a written protest. But Mr Tams, an official, shouted back: 'We have ruled the *Puritan* out; if you choose to sail the race you are free to do so.'

After more questioning the committee were asked by a member of *Genesta*'s crew: 'Will you give us time to rig up a spinnaker boom for a bowsprit?' But while the committee were deliberating on this point, Sir Richard Sutton put a sudden end to the discussion by saying: 'We are very much obliged to you, but we don't want it in that way. We want a race; we don't want a walkover.' This decision was quite satisfactory to the committee and their steam tug *Luckenbach* took the *Genesta* in tow and dropped her at Staten Island.

Both boats were repaired and ready to sail in time for the next race, which had been postponed until 11 September, but once again the wind had dropped away and the race had to be abandoned. On 14 September the race was at last started off Owl's Head, and as the tide carried the two boats past Long Island there was a mighty cheer for *Genesta* and her gallant young owner from the huge crowd gathered at the forts on either side of the Narrows.

Sadly, *Genesta* lost the race by over sixteen minutes and also the decisive second race held two days later. But although the British had failed yet again to produce the best boat, the magnanimous decision of Sir Richard Sutton not to accept a sailover set a high point in America's Cup sportsmanship.

An American correspondent writing about the event said: 'Hitherto we had regarded the challengers as ruffians, and as ruffians we had dealt with them, but now a wave of good feeling towards them has swept over the country.'

Sir Richard Sutton, wearing his favourite pink boating jacket, watches in horror as Genesta's long bowsprit lunges through Puritan's mainsail

Sir R. Sutton   torn mainsail

Genesta   Puritan

1886 MAYFLOWER defeats GALATEA

Mayflower	LOA: 100ft	Owner:
New York Yacht Club	LWL: 85ft 6in	General Charles J. Paine
	beam: 23ft 6in	Designer:
	draft: 9ft 9in	Edward Burgess
	draft with board: 20ft	Builder:
	displacement: 110 tons	George Lawley & Son
	sail area: 8600sq ft	Skipper:
		Martin Stone

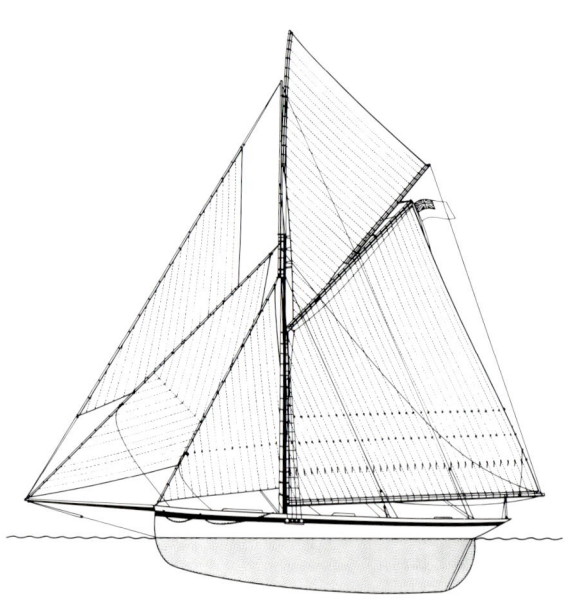

Galatea	LOA: 102ft 7in	Owner:
Royal Northern	LWL: 86ft 10in	Lt William Henn RN
	beam: 15ft	Designer:
	draft: 13ft 6in	J. Beavor-Webb
	displacement: 158 tons	Builder:
	sail area: 7505sq ft	J. Reed & Son
		Skipper:
		Dan Bradford

Lieutenant William Henn's challenge with *Galatea* in 1886 was probably more as a result of the designer's ambitions than those of the yacht's stolid owner. J. Beavor-Webb, who had designed *Genesta* the previous year, and who had convinced himself that his second boat was faster, was determined to pursue this double attempt regardless of a great deal of advice to the contrary.

Galatea had been named by Henn after a ship on which he had served in the Royal Navy. In Greek mythology, Pygmalion had carved a statue of a lovely damsel he called Galatea, and when he fell in love with it, Aphrodite had generously brought the statue to life. The 'tin frigate', as she was named, was loved almost as much, and certainly she was brought to life by Henn in every sense of the word. Henn and his wife, in contrast to any other challengers for the Cup before or since, lived on board *Galatea*. They had, moreover, surrounded themselves with a museum of Victorian bric-à-brac and a zoo consisting of several dogs, a lemur, and a monkey called Peggy, more of whom we shall hear later. *Galatea* would have been better nicknamed the 'Noah's Ark'.

Before leaving for America Henn, who was a cruising man by nature, entered his pride and joy in several races, but when she failed to win it was discovered that the lead had been incorrectly poured into her keel, which was full of holes and leaking. Once she had been repaired, he raced her three more times, but, when she had no better success, he decided without more ado to cross the Atlantic, arriving off Marblehead on 1 August 1886, after a leisurely trip of some thirty days.

The Yankees were waiting for him. Four American sloops had been prepared for the honour of defending, including *Puritan*, winner in 1885, *Priscilla*, which had not been nominated on that occasion, and two new boats, *Atlantic* and *Mayflower*. In general appearance *Puritan* and *Mayflower* were very much alike, and ultimately it was these two that were left to fight it out. Both constructed of wood, they had the same straight stem and the same graceful overhanging stern, and both were rigged like British cutters, except that their bowsprits did not reef. After losing her first three races, *Mayflower*, which had the finer entrance, proved superior in a head sea, and having won on 7 August at the Sow and Pigs, she never failed again.

Soon after his arrival, Henn joined the New York Yacht Club cruise from Buzzard's Bay. Painted white, with her 'Jack-yard' topsail and the rest of her well-cut canvas set, *Galatea* looked pretty in the light breeze, but any attempts by members of the Club to gauge her strength were foiled by her genial owner, who insisted at all times on towing a dinghy. Finally, when they tried to corner him, Henn threw down a challenge for any single-sticker to race him to Bermuda and back, but nobody called his bluff, or was confident enough to tackle the blue water.

General Charles Paine, who had also commissioned *Puritan*, engaged Captain 'Hank' Haff to skipper his new defender *Mayflower*, and as soon as the trial races were concluded, they hauled her out for a final polish. Paine, who was a stickler for crew discipline and efficient sail trimming, although confident that he had the leading skipper of that era, insisted on being on board for all her races, and when she was later, on 7 September, towed to the starting line off Owl's Head, he paraded *Mayflower* like a cavalry charger.

Galatea, on the other hand, had remained the sort of dark horse that might at any moment develop qualities unbefitting to the battlefield. Already the grog was being passed round, and it was not obvious that the British cutter had any intention of starting at all. But such was her owner's indifference that she had quietly gained a great deal of support, and when she surprisingly shot over the starting line in the lead, a cheer went up which was almost heard in Manhattan.

The weather had started foggy but cleared as the morning grew older, the sun breaking out as the two boats set off down the inside course into a light southerly breeze. Both yachts had crossed the line on the starboard tack, and as they headed for the narrows the strong flood tide set them to leeward and into the host of spectator craft, including a large anchored schooner. *Mayflower* had been pointing higher than *Galatea*, and fortunately for Haff he was able to luff round the obstacle and keep up his momentum. But for Beavor-Webb life was not so easy. Forced under the schooner's lee, he was badly blanketed, and as *Mayflower* passed them, only Peggy, the monkey, seemed to know what to do, and leapt off along *Galatea*'s lengthy bowsprit, determined to lower the sails. She might just as well have done so.

When *Mayflower* eventually tacked for the *Sandy Hook* lightship, she was already well ahead, and as she rounded and broke out her big jib topsail, more than a hundred steam whistles sent her hurrying home to a comfortable win.

The second and deciding race was no different. *Galatea* seemed to slide off to windward, and *Mayflower*, with her more effective centreboard, won again by a wide margin. Henn, who was absent due to illness, had asked for the course to be shortened so that he could take part on his way to see the doctor, but the New York Yacht Club, saying that they were unable to change the rules, had refused. So, disappointed, he decided to keep his yacht in America for another season, winning few trophies, but enhancing his reputation for sportsmanship all the time.

Peggy waits to bring in the jib. The monkey was used to joining in on the ropes with the crew – Galatea's skipper considered she was descended from man!

Peggy

Mayflower   schooner   *Galatea*

1887
VOLUNTEER defeats THISTLE

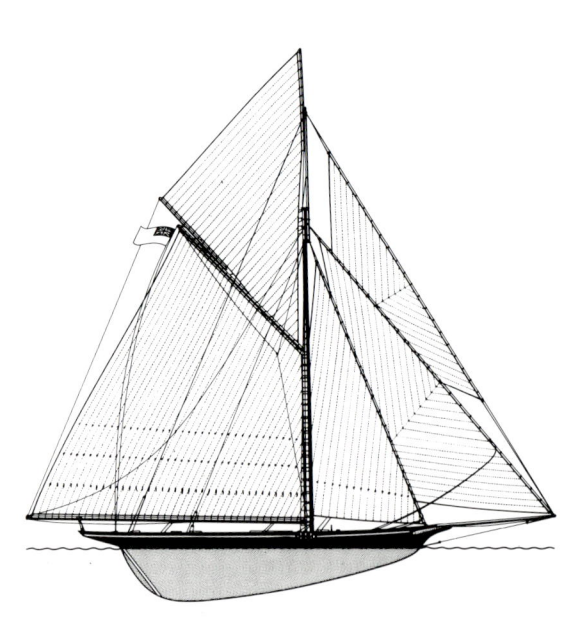

Volunteer		Owner:
New York Yacht Club	LOA: 106ft 3in	General Charles J. Paine
	LWL: 85ft 10in	Designer
	beam: 23ft 2in	Edward Burgess
	draft: 10ft	Builder:
	draft with board: 21ft	Pusey and Jones
	displacement: 130 tons	Skipper:
	sail area: 9271sq ft	Henry C. Haff

Thistle		Owner:
Royal Clyde	LOA: 108ft 6in	James Bell and syndicate
	LWL: 86ft 5in	Designer:
	beam: 20ft 3in	George L. Watson
	draft: 18ft 10in	Builder:
	displacement: 138 tons	D. & W. Henderson
	sail area: 8968sq ft	Skipper: John Barr

Vice-Commodore James Bell of the Royal Clyde Yacht Club was the next to lay his head on the chopping block. But when the Club's Secretary wrote to New York late in 1886 proposing a challenge with a boat 'about the size of *Mayflower*', the Cup committee simply sent back a curt reply, enclosing a copy of the Deed of Gift and stating that the challenge would only be considered when it was received in 'proper form'.

Although Bell and his syndicate were surprised by this rebuff, they decided that if the New York Yacht Club wanted to play it their way, then they would do likewise and continue with their plans regardless. As no British competitor had been built for the Cup for sixteen years, they had already sent the eminent Scottish designer, G. L. Watson, over to America to study all the latest tricks of the trade, and they now gave him carte blanche to go ahead and build the fastest yacht possible. Watson, who later designed the famous *Britannia*, was probably one of the most successful marine architects that Great Britain had ever produced, and because the Yacht Racing Association had in 1886 decided to change the old method of measurement for the 'length and sail area' rule, he was able to design a very different craft indeed. More beamy than her forebears, *Thistle* had a clipper bow, and was cut away at the forefoot to give a minimum of wetted surface when sailing in a light breeze. Built in utmost secrecy, she remained cloaked in tarpaulins until she hit the water, and Bell took particular pleasure in waiting until March to send in his formal challenge, giving the New York Yacht Club the minimum required information and little time to build a defender.

Undeterred, General Charles Paine again quickly picked up the gauntlet and, on account of his two previous successes, the defence was left entirely to him. He at once went to Edward Burgess and placed an order for a new sloop of approximately 85ft (26m). Constructed of steel, *Volunteer*, as she was named, was designed to carry more sail than any previous defender, and she was completed in the remarkably short time of sixty-six days.

Captain John Barr was put in charge of *Thistle*. Having won eleven of her fifteen trial races, easily outpacing *Genesta*, she left Gourock for New York on 25 July, accompanied for the first forty miles by the steam yacht *Mohican*, which was later to take over many of her supporters.

The Yankees had been baffled by all the secrecy surrounding *Thistle*, and when she docked after twenty-two days at sea, the New York *World* hired a diver to go down one dark night and explore the mysteries of her bottom. The result of his endeavours was a report of a keel so unlike that of any yacht afloat that Bell exclaimed, 'Did they really get a diver or was it a duck?'

On 2 September both boats were towed to the Erie Basin for official measuring, and when it was discovered that *Thistle* was nearly 1½ft (45cm) over her declared length, all hell was let loose. Bell should have been seriously embarrassed, for the water-line length of a yacht governs her maximum speed. But saying that her designer had been unable to give him more accurate information at the time of the challenge, he shrugged off the vociferous New York critics, asking what all the fuss was about as *Thistle* would be penalised on handicap. Eventually George Schuyler, the last of the Cup's donors, had to step in and agree to let *Thistle* race, for many thought that she should have been disqualified.

Excitement was intense for the first of the two duels, but as the morning fog lingered over the course and obscured the heights of Staten Island, the start had to be postponed. It was the last time, as it happened, that the race was to be held on the Club's inside course, and down in the narrows an immense fleet had gathered to send the two boats on their way. *Thistle* made the most of the delay, and her skipper, Captain Barr, threading his way through the spectators, caused gasps of dismay as he dodged amongst their clumsy craft, seeming to find a breeze as if by magic. The stock of the *Volunteer* and General Paine, sitting quietly in her stern wearing his old straw hat, went down even lower when from the *Mohican*, whose deck was crowded with fair dames glorying in the colours of the *Thistle*, there came the skirl of the bagpipes and the pungent aroma of a haggis which her cooks were preparing in the galley.

Such was the scene off Owl's Head as the starting cannon boomed, and *Thistle*, first over the line, basked in a few moments of glory before being determinedly and decisively overhauled by her opponent.

The second race was sailed in a stiffer breeze, but both results were so devastating that one American correspondent put it nicely as follows:

The canny crew of Scotchmen told us to wait for rougher weather, and so we waited. Now they have had their fill, the sooner they get back to their spindles, their fraoches and their meres and leave yachting to those who understand it, the healthier it will be for their wallets and for the honor of Bonnie Scotland. For ignorance and deceit the owners and designers of the *Thistle* take the cake – we take the Cup.

It was not a pleasant ending to what was then a purely sporting occasion, and some supporters, bewildered by *Thistle*'s sudden lack of form, accused her skipper, who stayed on in America, of accepting bribes from the opposition. But others were full of sympathy, and before Bell's departure for Scotland he and Watson were both invited to a reception given in their honour by the New York Yacht Club.

Waiting for the fog to lift, *Thistle* shows off her paces while *Volunteer*, displaying a banner asking spectators to keep clear, nudges towards the starting line with the only true wind coming from the pipers!

bagpipes

Thistle　　　　　　　　　　　　　Volunteer　　　　　　　　　　　　　Mohican

1893 VIGILANT defeats VALKYRIE II

Vigilant
New York Yacht Club
LOA: 124ft
LWL: 86ft 2in
beam: 26ft 3in
draft: 13ft 6in
draft with board: 24ft
displacement: 96 tons
sail area: 11,272sq ft
Owner: C. Oliver Iselin and syndicate
Designer: N. G. Herreshoff
Builder: Herreshoff Mfg Co
Skipper: William Hansen

Valkyrie II
Royal Yacht Squadron
LOA: 117ft 3in
LWL: 86ft 10in
beam: 22ft 4in
draft: 16ft 4in
displacement: 95.3 tons
sail area: 10,042sq ft
Owner: Earl of Dunraven
Designer: George L. Watson
Builder: D. & W. Henderson
Skipper: William Cranfield

In the spring of 1889 a challenge was received by the New York Yacht Club from the Earl of Dunraven through the Royal Yacht Squadron. The challenge was accepted. But after prolonged correspondence the matter was dropped as the Squadron were not prepared to agree the terms laid down under the Deed of Gift for any future challenger. These stated that a number of specific dimensions of the challenger had to be submitted to the New York Yacht Club ten months before the first race of each series. A compromise was eventually reached limiting the information required to water-line length only, and the challenge was fixed for the autumn of 1893.

With the revised Deed of Gift, a new era of cup racing began. No longer could a competent but comfortable cruising yacht hope to compete successfully. Because of changes in time allowance a new breed of yachts came off the drawing-boards with ends drawn out to give them maximum water-line length when the boats were heeled over. The greatly increased sail area meant that it was necessary to fit deeper keels, but although the yachts became faster they also became wetter!

Lord Dunraven asked George Watson, who had also drawn the lines of *Thistle*, defeated by *Volunteer* in the Cup match of 1887, to design him a cutter to fit the new rules. *Valkyrie II* was about double the rating of her elder sister and she carried over 10,000sq ft (930sq m) of sail.

As soon as the challenge was accepted the yachtsmen of New York and Boston decided to club together and repulse the invader. No less than four new sloops were built and pitted against one another in order to choose the defender. After an exhausting battle, *Vigilant*, commissioned by a New York syndicate, was given the job. Constructed of bronze below the water-line and steel above, she had a hollow bronze centreboard 16ft (4.9m) long and a solid bronze rudder. She carried 1,000sq ft (93sq m) more sail than the challenger and twice the crew.

The *Valkyrie*'s racing spars arrived in America aboard the *Berlin* on 11 September 1893. The yacht, which was close behind, had already gained a formidable reputation in home waters by winning 12 out of her 21 races, showing her pretty stern to the Prince of Wales, aboard *Britannia*, on more than one occasion.

For the series a new type of start had been implemented that is still used today. Previously, yachts were timed as they crossed the line during a two-minute handicap period following the starting gun. Now the gun was to signal the official starting time, which made for sharper competition.

The first race took place on 7 October over a 30-mile windward and leeward course from the *Sandy Hook* lightship. The race was an unsatisfactory test for both vessels due to the fickle wind and *Vigilant*, sailed by her designer, Nathaneal G. Herreshoff, finished well ahead.

Valkyrie was again beaten squarely in the second race with a freshening breeze, and the Yankee fears that she would be a demon in light airs and a devil in a blow seemed to be ill-founded. However, as it turned out, this prophecy nearly came true.

After the next contest had been declared void due to lack of wind, the decisive race was sailed on Friday 13 October. On that memorable morning the wind was once more piping in high from the east, and when the yachts arrived off the *Sandy Hook* lightship the sea was already wildly awake. The date decreed that an accident was inevitable and it was not long before *Valkyrie* was in trouble with a broken pulley-block. *Vigilant*, believing that her adversary was taking a reef in her mainsail, mistakenly followed her example.

On the outward beat the sky darkened. Crouched against the spray as *Vigilant*'s sharp bow cut through the grey water, her seventy crew members were now amazed to see *Valkyrie* making considerable progress to windward. When *Vigilant* rounded the final mark *Valkyrie* was ahead by almost two minutes, but as she steamed off down wind towards the finish, disaster struck. While the *Valkyrie*'s crew were hoisting the spinnaker, the sail split clean down the middle.

Herreshoff, seizing the advantage and casting away all caution, immediately ordered the reef in the mainsail to be shaken out. But he need not have bothered. As a man leapt along *Vigilant*'s boom, a mighty squall came up from astern and hit the black yacht ahead of them so hard that her reserve light-weather calico spinnaker, which had already fouled the rigging, exploded in tatters. *Vigilant*, staggering under a huge spread of canvas, stormed past.

Although *Vigilant* won the match, she gained the last race by only forty seconds on corrected time. *Valkyrie*'s performance on the wind was therefore to make many tongues wag. The advantages of a deeper keel over the traditional American centreboard undoubtedly contributed to a change in the underwater profile of future defenders.

Moments after the sudden squall had blown Valkyrie's second light-weather spinnaker to shreds a crew member, having cut the reef points, is helped down from Vigilant's boom as she storms past, in danger of losing her mast

Valkyrie II   *Vigilant*

1895 DEFENDER defeats VALKYRIE III

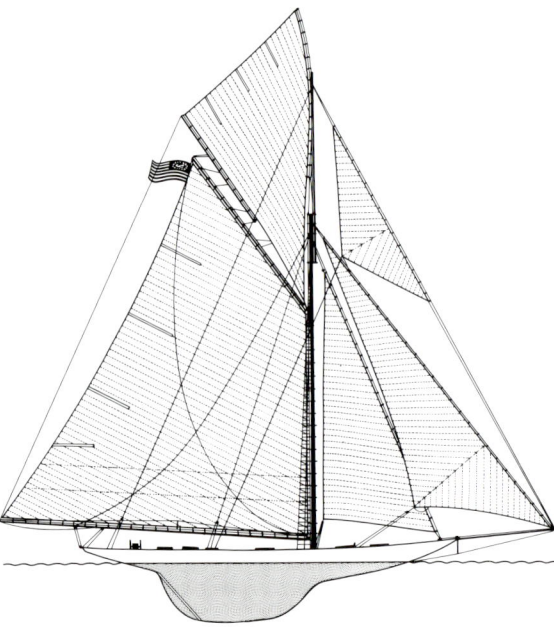

Defender	LOA: 123ft	Owner:
New York Yacht Club	LWL: 88ft 6in	C. Oliver Iselin,
	beam: 23ft	J. P. Morgan and
	draft: 19ft	William K. Vanderbilt
	displacement: 100 tons	Designer:
	sail area: 12,602sq ft	N. G. Herreshoff
		Builder:
		Herreshoff Mfg Co
		Skipper:
		Henry C. Haff

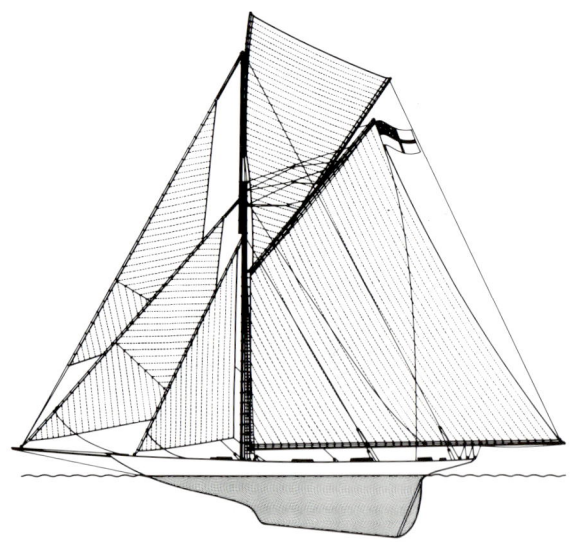

Valkyrie III	LOA: 129ft	Owner:
Royal Yacht Squadron	LWL: 88ft 10in	Earl of Dunraven and syndicate
	beam: 26ft 2in	Designer:
	draft: 20ft	George L. Watson
	displacement: 101.5 tons	Builder:
	sail area: 13,028sq ft	D. & W. Henderson
		Skipper:
		William Cranfield

The Earl of Dunraven, discontented with the results of the Cup match in 1893, decided with a number of friends, including the Earl of Lonsdale, to challenge again in 1895. He had no difficulty in arranging a series of five races with the New York Yacht Club to be held during September, and he asked George Watson to design a new yacht for him, to be called *Valkyrie III*.

A syndicate, managed by Oliver Iselin, was quickly formed in New York to finance a sole defender, to be named *Defender*, and the 'Wizard of Bristol', the great 'Nat' Herreshoff, was entrusted with the job of building her.

As it turned out both yachts were remarkably similar, although Herreshoff saved weight by using aluminium for *Defender*'s topsides. A few years later this experiment proved to be disastrous when electrolysis set in and she literally melted away. She was, however, to be a fine racing boat, and was the first in America to be fitted with a fin keel and not a centreboard.

Valkyrie, commanded by Captain Cranfield and assisted by Captain Sycamore, arrived in New York with only three weeks to spare and her owner immediately embarked on negotiations with the Yacht Club, which although at first amicable, soon were to brand Dunraven as England's most unsporting nobleman.

Dunraven, warned that Captain Haff on *Defender* might secretly add ballast, thus increasing speed by lengthening her water-line, insisted that the yachts be measured before each contest. Although the committee took steps to comply, *Valkyrie* could not be measured before the first race, and when she lost, all Dunraven could do was accuse *Defender*'s syndicate of malpractice, but without a shred of evidence.

From the outset Dunraven had also been worried, not without cause, by the proximity of the huge fleet of boats carrying an estimated fifty thousand spectators. The year before in Scotland *Valkyrie II*, his previous challenger, had been sunk, and a sailor had been killed, while trying to avoid a spectator craft. Dunraven had been at the helm, and he was determined that it should not happen again. He asked the committee to move the race to the less crowded waters off Marblehead, but they stated that the course could not be changed.

At least on this count Dunraven was correct. Despite all efforts by the committee to clear the spectators, the start of the second race was a shambles. As *Valkyrie* and *Defender* made for the line, a large steamer, the *Yorktown*, blundered across their bows, cutting between them, and when the two contestants came together again, they seemed about to collide.

Valkyrie was to weather of *Defender* and just before they reached the line 'Siccy' Sycamore at the helm of *Valkyrie*, seeing that he would hit *Defender* if 'Hank' Haff, who had the right of way, held his course, luffed up. As *Valkyrie* turned, the end of her boom raked *Defender*'s deck and snatching her starboard shrouds from the crosstrees it snapped the topmast stay with a sound like a pistol shot. *Defender*'s topmast bent like a bow, and Haff, whose first reaction had been to bear away, then spun her head to wind as Mr Iselin hoisted the red protest flag.

Fortunately the topmast seemed to be in no danger of falling, and by rigging a temporary stay, Haff, much to the spectators' amazement, was able to pursue the *Valkyrie*, who needless to say had not stopped to help, less than two minutes later. But without her jib topsail, which wisely had been stowed, and with her topmast leaning heavily to port, *Defender* was fighting at impossible odds, and it was to her credit that on corrected time she was only beaten at the finish by forty-seven seconds.

In acknowledging Mr Iselin's protest, the committee, already faced by a tense situation, did not hesitate in awarding him the race: 'We find that the *Valkyrie III* bore down upon the *Defender* and fouled her by the swing of her main boom when luffing to straighten her course.' Dunraven thought otherwise, and when Iselin chivalrously offered a resail, he ungraciously declined. He also wrote a letter to the Cup committee complaining about the broken water on the course caused by the washes of the excursion fleet.

By the third race it seemed that the public had taken notice and as much clear water had been allowed to the contenders as was reasonable. But there was something puzzling about the beautiful yachts waiting to take the stage. Whereas *Defender* had set a vast club topsail on her new spar, *Valkyrie*'s topsail remained tightly 'stopped'. Unknown to the media, Dunraven had written again to the committee saying that although they had failed to guarantee him a clear course, at least they could declare the race void if the competitors were obstructed. This request, later described by the chairman of the committee as absurd, was received too late and was never answered. Dunraven, in furious mood, failed to set his sails, and although when the starting gun boomed *Valkyrie* crossed the line, she immediately recrossed it and dropped her racing flag.

On returning to England, the Earl, finding that he had been slated by the press, had one last dig at the New York Yacht Club, of which he was an honorary member. In an article published in *The Field* that November, Dunraven specifically charged that *Defender* had added ballast before the first race, thus forcing the Club into holding an official enquiry. Treating the Earl with extreme courtesy, the enquiry judged that 'the subject of this investigation had its origin in a mistake' and the crew of *Defender* were blameless. When Dunraven failed to apologise to the Club, he was expelled.

The crippled *Defender*'s topmast, with the red protest flag already flying, leans backwards to her port side

bent topmast

committee boat　　　　　　　Valkyrie III　　　　Yorktown　　　　Defender

1899 COLUMBIA defeats SHAMROCK

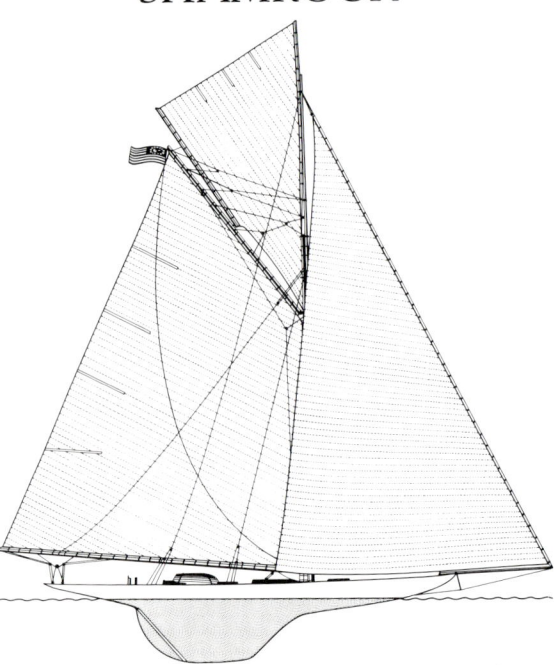

Columbia
New York Yacht Club
LOA: 131ft
LWL: 89ft 8in
beam: 24ft
draft: 19ft 3in
displacement: 102 tons
sail area: 13,135sq ft
Owner:
C. Oliver Iselin,
J. P. Morgan and
E. D. Morgan
Designer:
N. G. Herreshoff
Builder:
Herreshoff Mfg Co
Skipper:
Charles Barr

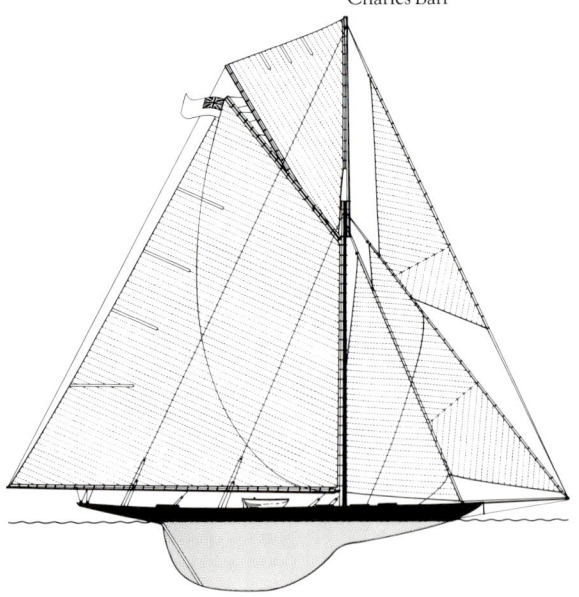

Shamrock I
Royal Ulster
LOA: 128ft
LWL: 87ft 8in
beam: 25ft
draft: 20ft 3in
displacement: 135 tons
sail area: 13,492sq ft
Owner:
Sir Thomas Lipton
Designer:
William Fife, Jr
Builder:
Thornycroft & Co
Skipper:
Archie Hogarth

The Earl of Dunraven's withdrawal from the Cup races in 1895 was to damp the enthusiasm of British yachtsmen for some time. It surprised even the most brazen of them when, two years later, it was rumoured round the bars that a challenge was about to be made by the Marquis of Dufferin through the Royal Ulster Yacht Club. The Marquis was indeed well qualified, for the 1876 challenger *Countess of Dufferin* had been named after his wife during his term as Governor-General of Canada, but by 1898 it was apparent that he had instead found a sponsor, the greatest diplomat of them all, Sir Thomas Lipton.

Lipton had come from a humble background and as a boy had worked for four years at several jobs in America. At nineteen he had started his own grocery business and now, at the age of fifty, his fortune had made him famous throughout the world. His friendship with the Prince of Wales, who had been greatly upset by the Earl of Dunraven's behaviour in 1895, was not disconnected with the new challenge, and, as expected, Lipton was soon to patch up relations with the Americans. Asked one day if his time as a boy in America had been the secret of his success, he replied, 'Bless yer, success with the ladies – yep!' Although he owned a luxury steamer, the *Erin*, he had never sailed a yacht in his life, but his enthusiasm for the game lasted a further thirty-one years, during which time he was to make no less than five attempts to win the cup for the Royal Ulster Yacht Club.

Lipton's cutter *Shamrock* was designed as a pure racing yacht by William Fife and constructed at Thornycroft's in England. Born to Irish parents in Glasgow, Scotland, Lipton had been determined to challenge with an Irish boat, but he was unable to find a yard in Ireland capable of building to such radical requirements. He was no luckier with her crew, for they too had to be recruited in Scotland and southern England. Only *Shamrock*'s name, her club and her fresh green paint eventually linked her with Ireland, and the twinkle in her owner's smiling Irish eyes.

Although *Shamrock*'s lines were kept a closely guarded secret, her adversary, *Columbia*, commissioned by C. Oliver Iselin, Edwin D. Morgan and the great Commodore J. Pierpont Morgan, proved herself well ahead in the quickening world of innovation. Pierpont Morgan, then perhaps the most influential man in America, had recently presented the New York Yacht Club with a plot of land on West 44th Street on which to build their new headquarters, and for him buying a yacht was no greater investment than buying a leg of mutton. But his intentions were more ambitious.

Permission was given for *Shamrock* to be towed across 'the pond' by the *Erin*, although she sailed eventually under jury rig, and Lipton arrived in New York by liner to a tremendous welcome. His yacht was immediately prepared for battle and quickly impressed the opposition with her speed. One account at the time said: 'The *Shamrock* yesterday gave a complete and remarkable performance. She is without doubt the fastest reaching yacht ever built.'

Columbia had the 1895 winner, *Defender*, as a trial horse to compete against throughout the summer, and there was no doubt that she was the better tuned yacht when the first race was held, after endless delays, on 16 October. *Shamrock* failed to carry her great 'Jack-yarder', although the wind was not strong, and, when she lost by more than ten minutes, it was obvious that she was far too tender.

The second race, held in a twelve-knot breeze, proved the point. Soon after the start *Shamrock*'s topmast snapped clean off, and her huge club topsail collapsed like a falling church steeple. The rules stated that the uninjured vessel should sail out the race, and *Columbia* scored her second win. Amazingly, *Shamrock* was back in the chase by the following morning.

The final race was held along the Jersey shore. Although several of the spectator boats had melted away due to further postponements caused by the weather, many of those craft that remained showed their appreciation of Lipton's sportsmanship by flying his colours. The run down to the mark was described by one American writer as 'the finest fifteen mile run in international yachting history', and as the two craft swept along together, like two beautiful ladies in their crinolines, a shout went up for the Irish grocer's gallant crew. As they approached the mark, *Columbia* finally edged ahead, and under the expert touch of Captain Charles Barr, later regarded by the American public as almost unbeatable, she turned the stake-boat better than *Shamrock* and increased her lead at the finish to over six minutes.

Columbia had undoubtedly been crewed better than *Shamrock*, although Captain 'Archie' Hogarth on *Shamrock* had been ably assisted by Ben Parker, skipper of the German Emperor's schooner *Meteor II*. *Shamrock*'s rig had also let her down, and the practicality of such out-and-out racing machines now raised many questions. Certainly there seemed scant hope for a design of yacht that could face little more than a puff of wind.

The challenge was to be remembered more for the arrival of one of the most honourable and persistent players in the history of the America's Cup, and for the departure, at least temporarily, of much of the acrimony that had surrounded it. Before he left for England, Lipton was elected an honorary member of the New York Yacht Club.

Many craft fly Lipton's colours, 'the Shamrock', in recognition of his great sportsmanship

flying 'the Shamrock'

Columbia   Shamrock

1901 COLUMBIA defeats SHAMROCK II

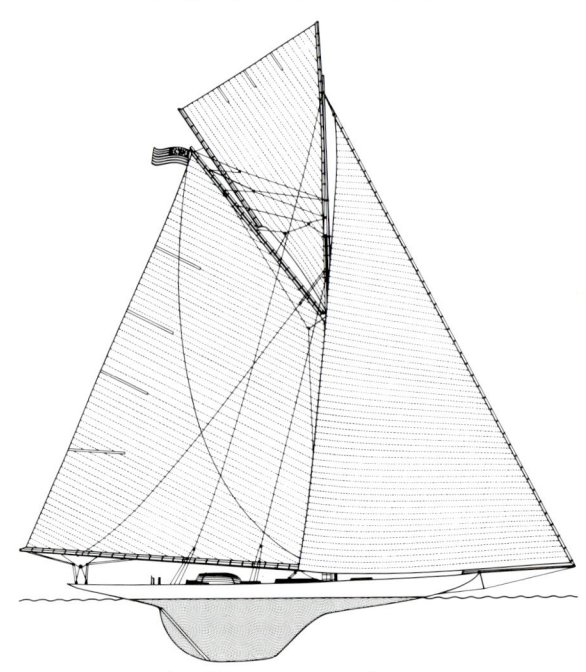

Columbia
New York Yacht Club
LOA: 131ft
LWL: 89ft 8in
beam: 24ft
draft: 19ft 3in
displacement: 102 tons
sail area: 13,135sq ft
Owner: C. Oliver Iselin, J. P. Morgan and E. D. Morgan
Designer: N. G. Herreshoff
Builder: Herreshoff Mfg Co
Skipper: Charles Barr

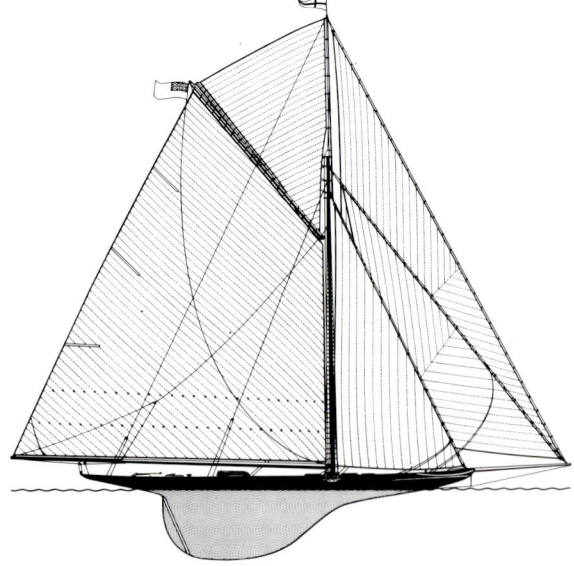

Shamrock II
Royal Ulster
LOA: 137ft
LWL: 89ft 3in
beam: 24ft 6in
draft: 21ft 3in
displacement: 129 tons
sail area: 14,027sq ft
Owner: Sir Thomas Lipton
Designer: George L. Watson
Builder: Wm Denny & Bros
Skipper: E. A. Sycamore

Directly the 1899 challenge was concluded, Sir Thomas Lipton announced that he would make a second attempt at seizing the Cup. He asked George Watson, the leading British designer, who had made his name with the brilliant cutter *Britannia* and with the previous challengers *Thistle* and the two *Valkyries*, to build him a new boat, *Shamrock II*. Watson set about the task with determination, and by tank testing scale models for the first time in sailing history, he was able to launch the most extreme type of racing hull that had yet been seen.

By 1901 the New York Yacht Club had held the America's Cup for so long that they believed that they alone had the right to defend it. It was therefore most upsetting to them when a Bostonian self-made multimillionaire, Thomas W. Lawson, decided to make his own bid for the honour without being elected a member of the Club. A furious row ensued when it was discovered that he had, unknown to them, commissioned a brute of a yacht, aptly christened *Independence* to carry the stars and stripes, and they set out to bring him to heel. But they need not have bothered. *Independence*, which had cost Lawson $200,000, had been built to unwieldy proportions and, although she proved to be very fast in certain directions, it was often difficult to steer her on any heading whatsoever! Arriving off Newport for the trial races she had to retire for a new rudder to be fitted, and on her return met such heavy weather that her plates started, she filled with water, and never sailed satisfactorily again. Before the Cup match had been decided she had already been sold as scrap.

Two other yachts, the 1899 defender *Columbia* and the new Herreshoff-designed *Constitution*, were left to battle it out for the right to represent their country, and it was probably only due to her poorly cut sails that *Constitution*, built with weight-saving web frames, narrowly lost.

Shamrock, constructed of a new light alloy called immadium, had been designed, regardless of the lessons learned with *Shamrock I*, to carry an immense amount of canvas, but before she left England her mast was found to be insufficient for the task. One day, when King Edward VII was aboard, it crashed down, and although in falling it caused little more trouble than to extinguish the gentlemen's cigars, the Cup race had to be postponed for a month while she fitted stronger spars.

Her hull having also been suitably strengthened with struts and stringers, she was eventually towed across the Atlantic by Lipton's steam yacht *Erin* at the end of July, but not before there had been a violent quarrel with some of the crew of *Shamrock I*, who refused to sail on the new boat unless they received better remuneration.

Shamrock was larger than *Columbia* and she carried 800sq ft (74sq m) more sail than her opponent. But through clever rigging of the peak halyard block, she avoided being heavily penalised on handicap, and when it was heard that she had exceeded fourteen knots during trials, the Yankees were extremely worried.

One fear had been laid to rest, however. In 1896, as a direct result of the notorious Dunraven affair of the previous year, the New York Yacht Club had managed to get an Act of Congress passed which gave the Treasury the task of controlling the errant spectator craft, and they had without more ado hired the Navy. The six revenue cutters and six torpedo boats detailed for the job were commanded by 'Fighting Bob' Evans, a hero of the Spanish–American War, who, learning from the previous challenge, resorted to the simple but effective method of dealing with offenders by firing a shot over their bows!

Although the races that followed found no place in the history books, they were remarkably close by any standards. In the first contest *Columbia* passed *Shamrock* on the homeward leg of the 30-mile course, winning by just over a minute, and the second match, held over a triangular course from the *Sandy Hook* lightship, was almost a repeat performance. With her lee rail buried, and her crew lying flat on the deck to windward, *Columbia* forged past *Shamrock* only a few miles from the finish, winning within seconds of the previous margin. But the third race was to be the most gripping of them all.

The breeze, blowing that day at about ten knots, was expected to favour *Shamrock* again, and after a slow start down the 30-mile leeward and windward course which had been set, she soon nosed ahead. But once more her two captains, Wringe and Sycamore, failed to press home their advantage, and as they approached the finishing line, the experienced Charlie Barr, at the helm of *Columbia*, caught them and mercilessly wore them down, crossing just two seconds behind *Shamrock* but forty-one seconds ahead on corrected time. It was the closest race in the annals of the America's Cup, and it was surprising that in the end little more than three minutes separated the two boats over 90 miles of battle.

Shamrock was left behind by Lipton at the Erie Basin and sadly was broken up only two seasons later, in the year of his subsequent challenge. Although she had failed to win a single match, she had proved herself to be a fast lady, and had almost certainly lost due to the superiority of the American helmsman.

Shamrock is almost caught at the line by *Columbia* as torpedo boats push back the excited spectators gathered on every type of craft

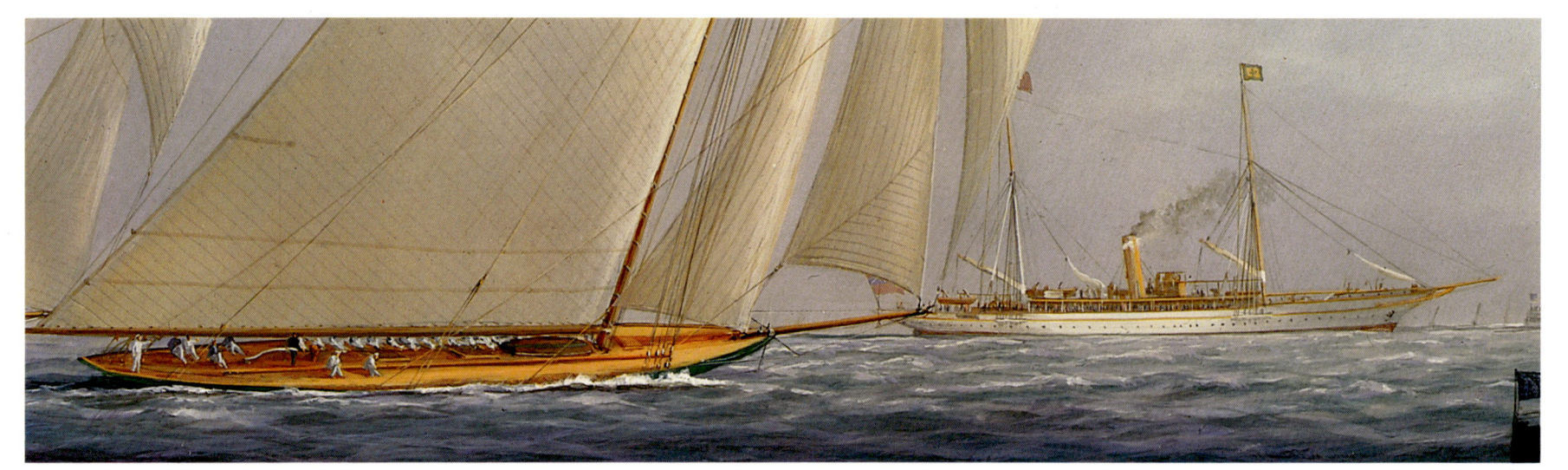

Capt Wringe on the tiller   Erin

Columbia   Shamrock II   torpedo boat

1903
RELIANCE defeats SHAMROCK III

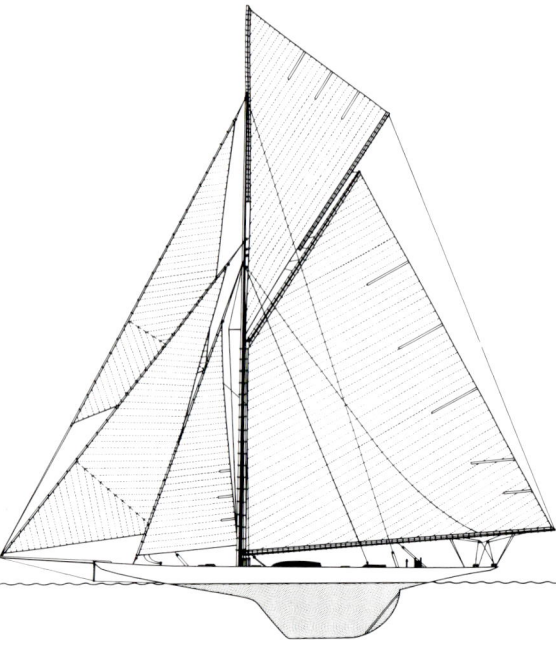

Reliance	LOA: 143ft 8in	Owner:
New York	LWL: 89ft 8in	C. Oliver Iselin and
Yacht Club	beam: 25ft 8in	syndicate
	draft: 20ft 6in	Designer
	displacement: 140 tons	N. G. Herreshoff
	sail area: 16,159sq ft	Builder:
		Herreshoff Mfg Co
		Skipper:
		Charles Barr

Shamrock III	LOA: 134ft 4in	Owner:
Royal	LWL: 89ft 10in	Sir Thomas Lipton
Ulster	beam: 26ft 6in	Designer:
	draft: 20ft 6in	William Fife, Jr
	displacement: 139 tons	Builder:
	sail area: 14,154sq ft	Wm Denny & Bros
		Skipper:
		Robert Wringe

Encouraged by the close-fought America's Cup contest of 1901 when neither boat held a significant advantage, Sir Thomas Lipton, having waited a decent interval for other challengers to come forward, put in his third bid in five years. 'In thus desiring an opportunity of making a third attempt to obtain possession of the America's Cup I hope I may not be deemed importunate or unduly covetous of the precious trophy so long and so securely held in trust by the New York Yacht Club', he wrote in his personal letter of 7 October 1902 accompanying the challenge submitted by the Royal Ulster Yacht Club. The New York Yacht Club agreed terms similar to those of 1901, and stated that the winner would be chosen from five races commencing August 1903.

Lipton's new boat, to be christened *Shamrock III*, was drawn for him by William Fife, the designer of the first *Shamrock*, and was given almost the maximum permitted water-line length of 90ft (27.5m). She was built of nickel steel coated with a much improved surface of white enamel, and for the first time for a British challenger, was equipped with a wheel instead of the traditional tiller. American helmsmen had been steering this way for years.

As soon as Lipton's challenge was accepted, a syndicate of New York millionaires, headed by William Rockefeller and Cornelius Vanderbilt, gave 'Nat' Herreshoff the job of building a radical new boat to an unlimited budget. The famous yard took the syndicate at their word and produced *Reliance*, the largest and most impressive yacht ever to take part in the America's Cup.

Reliance was a giant. Although her water-line length was within the rules, huge overhangs at bow and stern gave her, when heeled over with the lee rail under, a length of more than 130ft (40m) and therefore a great potential speed advantage over the challenger. She was topped with a steel mast which towered 196ft (60m) into the sky, and carried over 16,000sq ft (1,500sq m) of canvas, some 2,000sq ft (190sq m) more than the *Shamrock*. Her mainsail alone weighed 1½ tons (1,500kg), and to make handling easier her decks were dotted with winches. Constructed of tobin bronze, her hull was said to have cost no less than $175,000.

Lipton mistakenly, as he afterwards admitted, chose as his trial horse *Shamrock I*, the 1899 challenger, which although in better condition than *Shamrock II*, the 1901 challenger, was probably slower. Then at enormous expense he had both yachts, each with a crew of forty-one men, towed across the Atlantic to the Erie Basin, where *Shamrock II* was still moored! But at least it was the first time in America's Cup history that a challenger had another friendly yacht to tune up with.

Reliance, sailed by the experienced Charlie Barr with a vast crew of Scandinavians, many of whom worked below decks hauling in the sheets and trimming the backstays, quickly established her superiority over all the other prospective defenders. But, because of her shallow dish-shaped hull, she also proved to be tender in a blow, and the race committee decided not to take any chances and to amend the rules by banning racing in severe weather. When the third race in the series was subsequently postponed for this reason, it must have caused many old 'salts' to turn in their graves.

The first two contests, which were sailed on the outside America's Cup course south of Long Island starting at the *Sandy Hook* lightship, were both won by *Reliance* without difficulty, although she was forced, because of her measurements, to give *Shamrock* nearly two minutes handicap over the 30 miles. Captain Wringe, with Captain Bevis of *Shamrock I* at his side, sacrificed part of this handicap in the second race when *Shamrock* was late starting and this was repeated in the third race, eventually held after a delay of ten days.

Barr sailed the third race superbly, leaving *Shamrock* on every tack to the outer flag. By the weather mark *Reliance* had a lead of more than eleven minutes, but, before *Shamrock* could round the marker boat and set a course for home, the wind backed two points and brought a bank of fog rolling down on them from the south-east. Shut out, *Shamrock*'s navigator soon lost his direction, but *Reliance*, as she was narrowly missed by a spectator craft, managed to pick up the distant siren of the lightship and head towards the finish.

At the finish nothing was known of the contestants until those on the committee boat found themselves dwarfed by a cathedral of sail as *Reliance*, flying a vast spinnaker, ghosted over the line and hoisted an American ensign to signify her overwhelming victory.

It was the last time such an immense yacht was to be seen in the America's Cup and subsequently the rules were rationalised to produce a more sensible boat capable of competing in any weather and at a more reasonable cost. No one had tried harder than Tommy Lipton 'to lift the auld mug' as he would say, and even the great sportsman himself admitted that losing so conclusively was the greatest disappointment of his life.

As a result the America's Cup was to be forgotten for over a decade. Not a single foreign yachtsman came forward with a challenge and although Lipton bravely put in a bid late in 1912, it was not until after the Great War had been fought in Europe that he was, for the fourth time, able to come to grips again with the New York Yacht Club.

Reliance drifts on towards the finish as her vast crew listen for the sirens and Shamrock gets lost in the fog

Charlie Barr at the helm

spectator craft   *Reliance*   *Shamrock III*   stake-boat

1920
RESOLUTE defeats SHAMROCK IV

Resolute
New York Yacht Club
LOA: 106ft 4in
LWL: 74ft 11in
beam: 21ft 1in
draft: 13ft 9in
displacement: 99 tons
sail area: 8775sq ft

Owner: Henry Walters and syndicate
Designer: N. G. Herreshoff
Builder: Herreshoff Mfg Co
Skipper: Charles Francis Adams

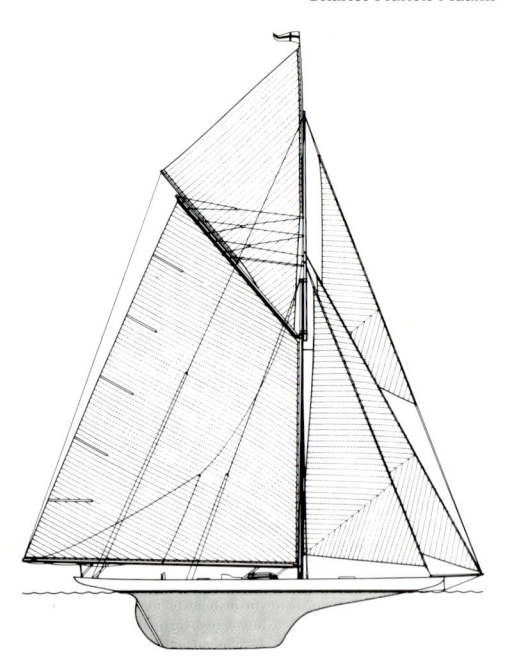

Shamrock IV
Royal Ulster
LOA: 110ft 4in
LWL: 75ft
beam: 24ft
draft: 14ft
displacement: 97 tons
sail area: 10,459sq ft

Owner: Sir Thomas Lipton
Designer: Charles Nicholson
Builder: Camper & Nicholson
Skipper: William Burton

In April 1913 the indefatigable Sir Thomas Lipton once more challenged for the Cup through the Royal Ulster Yacht Club. The Cup committee were in no hurry to reply, and when they did, they reserved the right to defend the Cup the following year with any size of boat up to a maximum permitted 90ft (27.5m). Lipton, unhappy that there should be such latitude, was unimpressed by this unnecessary horseplay, but when he declared that his new boat was to be 75ft (23m) he was informed, surprisingly, that the proposed length of the Yankee defender was to be exactly the same.

Lipton moved south this time and turned to the brilliant Charles Nicholson to design the thirteenth challenger. She was an unconventional-looking craft with a long narrow entry, a 'Marconi' or socketed topmast, and an ultra-light deck made from specially imported Russian plywood. She was also the first British challenger to be fitted with a centreboard in her keel. But although Nicholson had considerable knowledge of designing sailing yachts, *Shamrock IV* was his first America's Cup boat, and as a result he made one disastrous error. After all Lipton's misgivings about the defender, the challenger embarrassingly turned out to be the larger yacht, and because she was to carry 700sq ft (65sq m) more sail than her rival, it meant that she had to give away an unprecedented time allowance of more than seven minutes.

That was not the only bad news. No fewer than three new boats had been built in America for the 1914 defence: *Vanitie*, a beautiful yacht designed by William Gardner, who had also been responsible for the famous schooner *Atlantic*; *Defiance*, commissioned by a New York Yacht Club syndicate; and *Resolute*, sponsored amongst others by the powerful team of J. P. Morgan and Cornelius Vanderbilt, and designed and built by the redoubtable Nat Herreshoff.

All this effort was to be in vain, however, for in mid-Atlantic Lipton's steam yacht *Erin*, which had *Shamrock* in tow, picked up a radio signal from a German cruiser that war had been declared. It was not a pleasant situation, but the gallant *Erin* completed her mission and, having delivered *Shamrock* to New York, she again braved the Atlantic, returning only to be placed by her owner at the disposal of the British Government.

Once the fighting was over and things had simmered down, Lipton re-opened negotiations. During the war his lovely *Erin*, the pride of his life, had been hit by a torpedo while serving as a hospital ship in the Mediterranean, and had gone down with the loss of six of her crew. It was a bitter pill, but at least *Shamrock* had survived.

The committee were now keen that the races should be held off Newport, but Lipton, believing that this was yet another ploy, disagreed and succeeded in blocking them. Apart from not knowing those waters, the distinguished grocer, who always had an eye for publicity, preferred not to be so cut off from the media, and he splendidly demonstrated this one day when he showed a party of blondes over *Shamrock* in front of the cameras. Afterwards some said that it was the only occasion on which he had ever been seen on board!

Two of the three original boats, *Resolute* and *Vanitie*, were again vying for the honour of representing the New York Yacht Club. In one race *Resolute*, helmed by the experienced amateur 'Charlie' Adams, lost her mast in a squall, but after it had been replaced with a metal one there was no stopping her, and she duly won the nomination.

Lipton had brought over his 23 Metre *Shamrock* as a trial horse. Although she had never raced for the Cup, William Burton, at the helm of *Shamrock IV*, found her presence invaluable. But like Adams, Burton, although a fine yachtsman, was not a professional, and he was hampered by endless bickering amongst the more presumptuous of his afterguard.

There were many people in the United States who wanted 'the ugly duckling', as *Shamrock* was nicknamed, to win, and when she turned out for the first race on 15 July, with her mast sheathed in a special streamlined covering, they knew she meant business. There was a stiff breeze blowing, and both yachts got off to a good start from the *Ambrose* lightship, but close to the finish *Resolute*'s throat halyard parted when she was in the lead, and Adams, much to the dismay of his supporters, retired.

It had been the first race taken by a challenger since *Livonia* won in 1871. However there was little glory in the achievement, and Sir Thomas was far from happy. But when in the following race, *Shamrock*, despite a torn balloon jib, crossed the line nearly nine and a half minutes ahead of her opponent, he cheered up considerably!

Having won two of the best of five races, *Shamrock* only needed one more. Thirty minutes after the start of the third race, again held on a windward and leeward course, she looked like getting it. However, as the breeze freshened, *Resolute*, pointing higher, began to close the gap and both crews started fighting for their lives. On each of the nineteen tacks Adams managed to take Burton's weather until by the end of the windward leg he was at last in the lead. But after the turn *Shamrock* slowly began to claw back the deficit, finishing just ahead, but sadly outside her time allowance.

The last two races were also won by *Resolute*, which was ultimately considered the faster boat, but it had been a magnificent struggle and the closest any challenger had ever been to winning the America's Cup.

In the third race *Shamrock IV* and *Resolute* battle it out as Burton and Adams, the first amateur skippers in the Cup's history, struggle for the advantage

The beak of the ugly duckling

Corsair III   Shamrock IV   Resolute

1930
ENTERPRISE defeats
SHAMROCK V

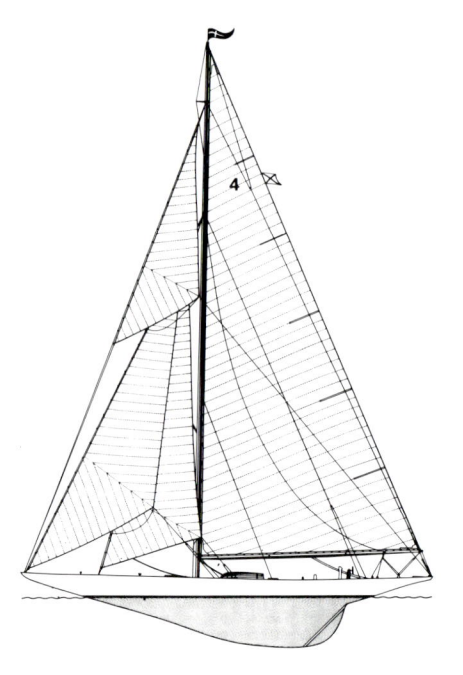

Enterprise
New York Yacht Club

LOA: 120ft 9in
LWL: 80ft
beam: 22ft 1in
draft: 14ft 6in
displacement: 128 tons
sail area: 7583sq ft

Owner: Winthrop Aldrich and syndicate
Designer: W. Starling Burgess
Builder: Herreshoff Mfg Co
Skipper: Harold Vanderbilt

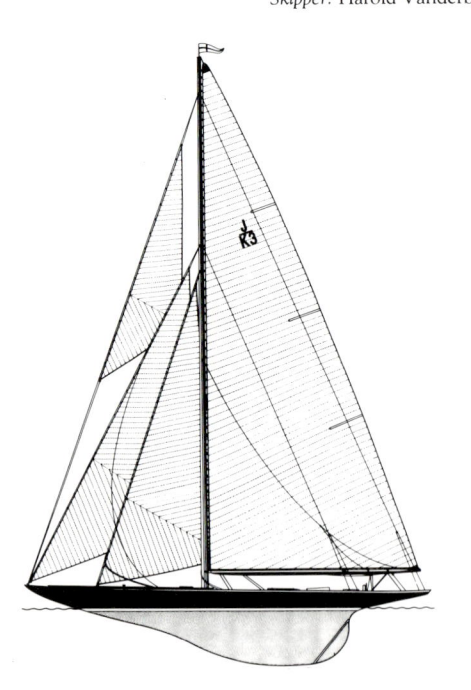

Shamrock V
Royal Ulster

LOA: 119ft 1in
LWL: 81ft 1in
beam: 19ft 9in
draft: 14ft 9in
displacement: 134 tons
sail area: 7540sq ft

Owner: Sir Thomas Lipton
Designer: Charles Nicholson
Builder: Camper & Nicholson
Skipper: Ned Heard

The great competitor Sir Thomas Lipton was approaching his eightieth birthday when he launched *Shamrock V*. Since 1920 so many advances had been made in light yacht construction that he had come to the conclusion that all further attempts at the Cup would be hopeless until the rules ensured that both yachts were built to the same degree of seaworthiness. The recently formed North American Yacht Racing Union had decided in 1927 to adopt the international rule of measurement for yachts over 48ft (14.5m), ensuring that in future certain classes of yachts would be built to race without handicap, and it was this that encouraged Lipton, two years later, to make his final desperate bid.

By 1929 the New York Yacht Club had also conformed, but they preferred that the America's Cup contestants should be measured under the more flexible universal rule. At the same time both sides welcomed the club's decision to race J-Class, and the Yankees, much to the delight of boat yards, proceeded to order four of them.

In total only ten true J-Class were ever built. Their high aspect ratio sails and towering masts gave them great power and awesome beauty, but they were so staggeringly expensive that by the end of the thirties even those with the deepest pockets could no longer afford them, being saved from the embarrassment of having to admit it only by the outbreak of World War II.

Shamrock V, designed to the new formula by Charles Nicholson, quickly earned praise on the British regatta circuit, and during her first season won an impressive fifteen races out of her twenty-two starts before leaving for America.

The four 'J's built in answer to Lipton's challenge, *Whirlwind*, *Weetamoe*, *Yankee* and *Enterprise*, cost more than half a million dollars each, but it was not the money that Lipton was up against; he had the bad luck to be confronted by two of the most determined characters in the Cup's history.

Harold S. Vanderbilt, great grandson of once the richest man on earth, 'The Commodore' Cornelius Vanderbilt, with his designer Starling Burgess, had set about defending the Cup with such cold and calculated resolve that he and his syndicate were almost to lose the support of the American people, so great was their love and respect for Sir Tommy. As a result, *Enterprise*, which had soon been chosen as the defender, was acknowledged to be the most exciting, innovative and perhaps romantic racing yacht ever built:

Your builder's soul and your captain's too,
Who loves your pure white sails
Against a background of pale blue;
And a wind that never fails.
You're like a dream ship, Enterprise,
A ghost you are in white;
A lovely vision in any eyes
That see you here tonight.
And so you rest beneath the stars
While silent their soft light gleams
On your white sails furled, and your lofty spars,
To make you a frame of dreams;
And I know you'll win most easily,
For you are our pride and best,
Enterprise, Champion of the Sea,
Star of the mighty West.
(From 'Enterprise', written for Harold S. Vanderbilt by Elmer Ellsworth Ford.)

It seemed, indeed, that *Enterprise*'s great mast almost reached the stars. Much lighter than *Shamrock*'s wooden spar and made of duralumin, its twelve sides had been fastened together by no fewer than 80,000 rivets, and to allow it to move it had been stepped in a steel sleeve filled with quicksilver. To complete the balancing act, the 'tin mast', as it came to be called, was held up by numerous stays, each monitored by a strain gauge. Burgess, who had been a leading aeronautical designer, had also lightened the yacht's hull with the help of special web frames, and her two dozen winches had all been carefully selected by weight. But what particularly amazed the opposition was that many of these winches were out of sight below-decks, where eight sailors, known as the 'black gang', worked to orders shouted through a hatch. Even more surprising, however, was the triangular-shaped 'Park Avenue' boom. Its flat top was wide enough for two men to walk along side by side, and using a series of horizontal tracks with coloured pegs it was possible to shape the mainsail for maximum efficiency. Efficiency was the word on *Enterprise* and her crew, who were drilled to perfection, all wore numbered jerseys to show their station.

It has been agreed that for the first time the races would be held off Newport, Rhode Island, as the 'J's were so tall that they could not pass under many of the bridges on the East River, but sadly for the New Englanders who turned out in their thousands to watch, their hero Tommy Lipton's boat never stood a chance. The first of the best of seven races was won by *Enterprise* by nearly three minutes, the second by nearer ten minutes, and only the third race provided any excitement at all.

Lipton, watching from his motor yacht *Erin*, saw *Shamrock* lead at the start only to be overtaken by *Enterprise* in a tacking duel. The wind was blowing up from the west and as *Shamrock*, two minutes astern on the starboard tack, ploughed uncomfortably into the head sea, her main halyard parted and her sail clattered to the deck. There was no way she could continue, and so Vanderbilt, unlike Sir Richard Sutton in 1885, sailed on to claim victory.

The fourth and deciding race was again won by *Enterprise*, and the grand old man, for the first time in his life, was heard to mutter, 'I can't win, I can't win'. Vanderbilt, writing later, could only attribute *Shamrock*'s defeat to badly set sails, inferior spars, and a certain lack of professionalism.

Enterprise carries on as a revenue cutter turns in Shamrock's direction

Mike Vanderbilt at the helm

Erin   *Enterprise*   *Shamrock V*

1934
RAINBOW defeats ENDEAVOUR

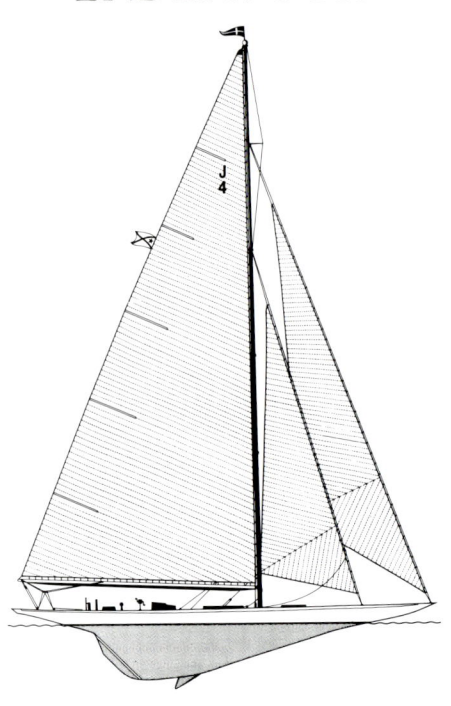

Rainbow
New York Yacht Club
LOA: 126ft 7in
LWL: 82ft 4in
beam: 21ft
draft: 14ft 6in
displacement: 141 tons
sail area: 7535 sq ft
Owner: Harold Vanderbilt and syndicate
Designer: W. Starling Burgess
Builder: Herreshoff Mfg Co
Skipper: Harold Vanderbilt

Endeavour
Royal Yacht Squadron
LOA: 129ft 8in
LWL: 83ft 3in
beam: 22ft
draft: 14ft 11in
displacement: 143 tons
sail area: 7561 sq ft
Owner: T. O. M. Sopwith
Designer: Charles Nicholson
Builder: Camper & Nicholson
Skipper: T. O. M. Sopwith

The Depression of the 1930s was to hit the yachting industry hard. But somehow the great boats survived, as they usually do, and by 1933 the order books were beginning to fill once more. The magnificent J–Class now ruled the waves, and they had been joined by *Shamrock V*, bought after the death of Sir Thomas Lipton by the distinguished aircraft manufacturer T. O. M. Sopwith. Sopwith, who was already one of the best amateur helsmen in England, decided at the end of the season to build a new boat and challenge for the America's Cup.

The New York Yacht Club accepted, but they also announced changes to the rules. Yachts in future would be expected to have crew's quarters, thus eliminating the below-decks mechanisation of *Enterprise*, the 1930 defender, and both competitors were to have identical J–Class ratings.

Sopwith approached the task more professionally than Lipton. The experienced Charles Nicholson was chosen to design the new yacht, and Frank Murdoch, an aeronautical engineer working with Sopwith, was asked to help with the rigging and other advanced features.

Endeavour, launched in April 1934, was acknowledged to be the most beautiful 'J' yet built. She was also such a superb racing machine that she was to come within an ace of winning the America's Cup for Great Britain.

The defender, *Rainbow*, was commissioned by 'Mike' Vanderbilt, who had defended the cup successfully with *Enterprise* in 1930, and headed a syndicate of seventeen patriotic millionaires. *Rainbow* was lucky to be chosen, for in trials she was almost defeated by *Yankee*, who was to make her name the following year racing in England.

Sopwith was meanwhile trying out a radical double-clewed, or quadrilateral, jib in the Solent. Later, he was to regret that he had not tested it further away from prying eyes, for within a few days the Americans were flying their own 'Greta Garbo' as they called it. *Endeavour* was towed to Newport, Rhode Island, by Sopwith's motor yacht *Vita*. But, before she left England, she suffered a disaster which almost certainly cost her the Cup. Her professional crew had gone on strike for more pay, and as a result Sopwith, in cavalier mood, had misguidedly replaced many of his men with amateurs.

The first two races were sailed in strong winds and rough seas, and *Endeavour* won both impressively. In the second race Sopwith, the first British owner to sail an America's Cup boat himself, beat the course record. *Endeavour*, accepted as being the faster boat, had already achieved more than any challenger – now all she needed was one more victory. The British were ecstatic.

The third race was again *Endeavour*'s, right until the final beat. Vanderbilt, believing the Cup had gone, went below and handed over the helm to Sherman Hoyt, a much respected and crafty sailor, who knew from past experience that Sopwith liked to cover his rival at all times. He luffed up into the light breeze, causing Sopwith to cover him by tacking twice. *Endeavour* lost momentum and the race. Sopwith and his crew were devastated, but they had a further chance.

In the fourth race the two boats nearly collided at the start. Both skippers thought the other was at fault, but neither flew a protest flag. *Rainbow* had a twenty-second lead crossing the starting line, but by the first mark *Endeavour* had already overtaken her. Then the inexperience of Sopwith's crew once again began to tell.

Sopwith had as his navigator a merchant navy officer called Paul who, although efficient at plotting a course across the Atlantic, had little knowledge of racing. Paul was now to direct Sopwith too far down wind, and by the time Sopwith realised the mistake, *Rainbow* was forging past. Sopwith quickly threw over the helm with the intention of forcing Vanderbilt to luff into wind and give way, as was allowed by the racing rules, in a desperate attempt to stop him passing.

Sherman Hoyt, who had been sitting on *Rainbow*'s spinnaker boom, reckoning that the two yachts were about to collide, shouted: 'Luff! Luff, Mike, for God's sake luff!' But Vanderbilt carried straight on.

Vanderbilt had risked everything. If the two boats had struck each other it would have been a disaster; but if Sopwith, now compelled to bear away, protested, and proved successfully that he would have hit *Rainbow* forward of the shrouds, Vanderbilt would lose the Cup.

As he approached the committee boat at the finish, over a minute behind *Rainbow*, Sopwith hoisted the red protest flag, according to British rules. But the race committee declined to consider the protest, saying that in America the flag had to be flown at the time of the foul. Later, the committee defended their decision by saying that *Endeavour* had already fouled *Rainbow* before the start, and if they were now forced to eliminate her, she would then be unable to disqualify her opponent.

Vanderbilt, hotly denying that he had been within thirty metres of *Endeavour*, went on to win the next two races and the America's Cup. But the incident caused a major controversy that has never been settled.

Sherman Hoyt, wearing his famous red pants, shouts at Vanderbilt to give way. (The incident has been painted from photographs taken by a spectator through a telescope. They are shown earlier in this book.)

Sherman Hoyt

T. O. M. Sopwith   *Endeavour*   *Rainbow*

1937 RANGER defeats ENDEAVOUR II

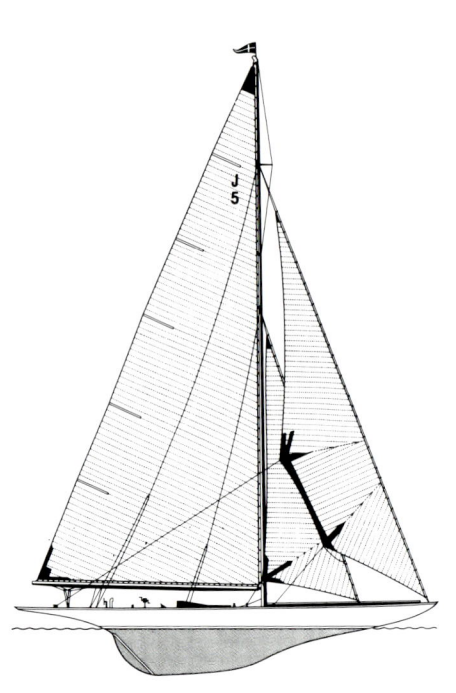

Ranger
New York Yacht Club
LOA: 135ft 2in
LWL: 87ft
beam: 21ft
draft: 15ft
displacement: 166 tons
sail area: 7546sq ft
Owner: Harold Vanderbilt
Designer: W. Starling Burgess and Olin J. Stephens
Builder: Bath Iron Works
Skipper: Harold Vanderbilt

Endeavour II
Royal Yacht Squadron
LOA: 135ft 9in
LWL: 87ft
beam: 21ft 6in
draft: 15ft
displacement: 163 tons
sail area: 7543sq ft
Owner: T. O. M. Sopwith
Designer: Charles Nicholson
Builder: Camper & Nicholson
Skipper: T. O. M. Sopwith

Sadly for the contestants, and for the boats' admirers, by 1937 the wonderful world of the J-Class was rapidly drawing to a close. T. O. M. Sopwith had ordered a new boat to challenge with in 1936, but had nearly been thwarted by a rival aircraft manufacturer, Sir Richard Fairey, who wanted to race the smaller and more practical American K-Class. The New York Yacht Club were not in favour, however, and Fairey's proposed yacht *Windflower* was never built, but it had been registered that the days of the elegant dinosaurs were numbered.

Because 1936 was the somewhat frantic year of the presidential election, Sopwith's challenge could not be entertained until the following season, giving him more time to get *Endeavour II*, which had already been twice dismasted, tuned up. Charles Nicholson had built a fine-looking yacht to the maximum water-line length of 87ft (26.5m), and because she seemed to be faster than her predecessor *Endeavour I*, which had so nearly got the better of Vanderbilt's *Rainbow* in 1934, it was believed in America that they had no suitable yachts likely to be able to beat her.

At first Mike S. Vanderbilt, who was determined to mount his third defence, tried to raise funds through a syndicate to be formed by the New York Yacht Club, but the economy being in poor health, no one came forward. There was little time to lose and so, untypically for a defender, he guaranteed the costs himself, estimated to be around $400,000. In another brave move he asked the young Olin Stephens, already acknowledged as one of the most successful yacht designers in the world, and Starling Burgess, who amongst other achievements had built the first seaplane, to design the new yacht jointly, a combination that resulted in the greatest 'J' ever built. Unlike *Endeavour*, *Ranger* was the product of extensive tank testing and, being constructed at the Bath Iron Works in Maine, she was the first defender for over forty years not to be completed by the Herreshoff yard in Bristol.

While *Ranger* was being towed from her builders, the rod rigging securing her duralumin mast started shaking loose, and as the crew hid below, the huge 165ft (50m) spar crashed down on the deck. But it was to be her only misfortune.

My mast is duralumin, but costlier than gilt,
The wind that fills my riggin' is a million dollar breeze,
From my bowsprit to my topsail, I am wholly Vander-built,
And I only go a-sailing in the most exclusive seas.
Redbook 1937

Exclusive as she was, she still had to prove herself in trials against the famous *Yankee*, owned by Gerard Lambert, and the previous two Cup winners, *Rainbow* and *Enterprise*. It was not asking much: of her thirteen starts she won all thirteen.

Endeavour II was towed across the Atlantic by a trawler in the company of *Endeavour I*, whose new owner Hermann Andreae had chartered her to Sopwith's business partner, Fred Sigrist, as a trial horse. She arrived slightly ahead of her sister, who had been forced to slip her tow in a gale and carry on under jury rig. Sopwith decided to sail the two boats in tandom and try out every combination of sails and spars until he was happy. Denied the chance of weighing up the challenger in formal trial races, the American press were distinctly unhappy.

Due to the controversy surrounding the 1934 match, when the contestants nearly collided, Vanderbilt, playing it carefully, was behind for the first two starts. The races were only notable for the margins by which *Ranger* won: in the first race by seventeen minutes and in the second race by more than eighteen minutes. As *Ranger* had been attacked by the press for these poor starts, in the third race Vanderbilt piled on the pressure, but won this time by less than five minutes.

By the fourth race the spectators, judging the result to be a foregone conclusion, had dwindled considerably, but overhead a Sopwith Pup, flown by an American enthusiast, swooped in salute of the great Englishman. With eleven minutes to go before the start, Vanderbilt fastened himself on *Endeavour*'s tail and, despite all Sopwith's attempts to shake him off, he was still there at the one-minute signal. It was clear that *Endeavour* would run out of room before the end marker, and so close were the boats that Rod Stephens, Olin's brother, was sent up to the stem-head to signal if *Ranger* could pass under *Endeavour*'s stern when she went for the line. Sopwith was in a cleft stick, and being unable to bear away, he took the only option left to him, crossing the line on the starboard tack just five seconds too early, the first America's Cup helmsman to have been put in that position.

Vanderbilt, starting three seconds late, sped off down the course as Sopwith gybed in a circle round the marker buoy and gave chase only seventy-five seconds adrift, losing this, the final race, by just three minutes. It was a good effort, for *Ranger* was, without question, a superstar. Of her thirty-seven races during her first and only season, she was to win all but two.

Although Sopwith maintained that *Endeavour II* was the faster of his two challengers, she was later forgotten as Sopwith launched on his third great endeavour (see introduction), and he never knew what became of her. *Endeavour I*, however, again surviving a hurricane on her return trip to England, was put to bed in a mud berth, and amazingly, after countless years, has been reborn. But sadly, unlike the sentimental British, the Americans at that time were more materialistic, and *Ranger* with all her relatives, destined for a more serious contest, was broken up and fed to the arsenals of war.

As a Sopwith Pup swoops overhead, *Endeavour II* is forced over the starting line by the mighty *Ranger*, five seconds too soon

America's Cup buoy   Sopwith Pup

Ranger   Endeavour II

1958 COLUMBIA defeats SCEPTRE

Columbia	LOA: 69ft 7in	Owner:
New York	LWL: 45ft 8in	Henry Sears and syndicate
Yacht Club	beam: 11ft 9in	*Designer*
	draft: 8ft 11in	Sparkman & Stephens
	displacement: 58,000lbs	*Builder:* Nevins
	(29 tons)	*Skipper:*
	sail area: 1825sq ft	Briggs Cunningham

Sceptre	LOA: 68ft 10in	Owner:
Royal	LWL: 46ft 6in	Hugh Goodson and
Yacht	beam: 11ft 9in	syndicate
Squadron	draft: 9ft 1in	*Designer:* David Boyd
	displacement: 61,152lbs	*Builder:*
	(30 tons)	Alex Robertson & Sons
	sail area: 1832sq ft	*Skipper:* Graham Mann

After his successful defence in 1937, Mike Vanderbilt, a master bridge player, was one of the first to recognise that the cards were stacked against the magnificent 'J's ever again competing for the America's Cup. So instead he had Olin Stephens design him a 12 Metre called *Vim*, a boat he was to win with many times during the 1939 regatta season in England. 'Twelves' had been around since 1907, but they were fine racing boats with impressive longevity. World War II put a stop to all further challenges for the Cup, however, and ultimately there was a gap of over twenty years before the British again got their act together – well almost!

During the intervening period, the longest in the Cup's history, much had changed. The great fortunes were now no longer great, and as by 1956 no new Cup yachts had been built, the Royal Yacht Squadron were asked by the Americans to recommend a more economical class for the future. Hoping for candidates, they chose the 12 Metre, then the largest racing yacht still attracting enthusiasm on both sides of the Atlantic, and later that year a new and fourth Deed of Gift was passed by the New York Supreme Court in order to adjust the rules. The minimum water-line length was changed to 44ft (13.5m), and the requirement that the challenger must sail to the races on her own bottom was deleted. (The rating, 'metre', was a formula of several different dimensions, and the length of the 'Twelves' was nearer 70ft (21m) over all.)

Unfortunately, partly due to the poor showing of their 'Twelves' at the 1952 Olympics, yachtsmen in Great Britain had already turned their energies more to ocean racers. It was lucky that a syndicate of nine patriots headed by the popular Devonian Hugh Goodson, and including Herman Andreae, owner of the 'J' boat *Candida* and subsequently *Endeavour*, and Sir Peter Hoare the banker, were encouraged enough to build a challenger.

Hugh Goodson invited 'Stug' Perry, who had won the silver medal with *Vision*, his 5.5 Metre, at the Melbourne Olympics, to act as technical advisor, and with Frank Murdock, Sopwith's brilliant assistant between the wars, they selected David Boyd from four aspirants to design the new yacht. *Sceptre* was then built at Alexander Robertson's yard in Scotland where Boyd was managing director. Unhappily Perry was later to resign.

Perhaps the best-kept secret of *Sceptre*'s design was her vast open cockpit. It was hoped that this would improve her performance by reducing deck weight, and, in providing the crew with a safe working area, it also lowered the centre of gravity. But later her critics were to say that it only increased wind drag, and the Americans would never have copied it any case.

Boyd's problem was that he had no decent plans to work from. There was only one man still alive who had designed a 12 Metre, Olin Stephens, and Olin was busy on the yacht he hoped would be chosen as the third *Columbia* to successfully defend the America's Cup. Sailed and part owned by Briggs Cunningham, who had crewed on *Vim* in 1939, *Columbia* soon asserted her authority over the other new boats *Weatherly* and *Easterner*, but found old *Vim* a harder nut to crack. The needle races which followed, ending in *Columbia*'s selection, contributed to her final victory, while *Spectre*, launched earlier during April, had only Owen Aisher's *Evaine* to box with. Worse still, on her arrival by steamer in New York during August, it was found that her American sparring partner, *Gleam*, was uncompetitive and happened to carry an engine!

Lieutenant Commander Graham Mann, *Sceptre*'s skipper, who had been Sailing Master on the Royal Dragon *Bluebottle*, winning a bronze at the Melbourne Olympics, now found himself ordering buckets to be dragged astern in order to slow *Sceptre* down. At least her crew, which unfortunately had not been picked until the end of June, thought that there might be some consolation in being a 'dark horse'. Poor *Sceptre*, although she seemed to prefer a blow, found that in the steep Atlantic swell her blunted bow section did her no justice, and a more fitting description would have been a 'rocking horse'!

The match itself was an anticlimax. The finer built *Columbia*, pointing higher and riding better, left *Sceptre* far behind, and won four straight races, watched on the first occasion by President Eisenhower from a destroyer.

The series had once again proved that no British challenger could succeed without adopting the professional approach of the Americans, whose designers took advantage of every innovation, and continued working on their boats throughout each match. In comparison, *Sceptre* was the result of a bold venture, carried out by enthusiastic amateurs. Although chosen from several tank-tested models, *Sceptre*'s lines were not the result of serious tank testing, and her sails, particularly her huge Herbulot spinnakers, were inappropriate for many of the conditions experienced. But Goodson and his syndicate had done a grand job by putting the America's Cup in the calendar again, and by building *Sceptre* they had probably, unwittingly, saved the 12 Metre class from almost certain death.

'The Moment of Truth'. The twenty-knot breeze, blowing at the start of the third race, gave Graham Mann, who had sailed well, some encouragement. But all hope vanished as *Sceptre* buffeted into the waves and *Columbia* romped away up wind

Graham Mann

Columbia   Sceptre

1962
WEATHERLY defeats GRETEL

Weatherly
New York Yacht Club
LOA: 66ft 10in
LWL: 46ft
beam: 11ft 10in
draft: 8ft 11in
displacement: 59,000lbs (30 tons)
sail area: 1850sq ft

Owner: Henry Mercer, Arnold Frese and Cornelius Walsh
Designer: Philip Rhodes
Builder: Luders
Skipper: Bus Mosbacher

Gretel
Royal Sydney Yacht Squadron
LOA: 69ft 5in
LWL: 45ft
beam: 11ft 10in
draft: 9ft
displacement: 60,480lbs (30 tons)
sail area: 1900sq ft

Owner: Sir Frank Packer and syndicate
Designer: Alan Payne
Builder: Lars Halvorsen
Skipper: Jock Sturrock

Sceptre's defeat in 1958 had left a nasty taste in the mouth, and so, determined to put matters right, two syndicates were formed in England with the intention of building better boats for 1962. But the next challenge was, as it happened, to come from an entirely different direction, and there were howls of protest when it was discovered that the New York Yacht Club had already agreed to defend the Cup against a surprise entry from the Southern Ocean. All the Royal Thames Yacht Club could do, after the Duke of Edinburgh had tried to help by suggesting a joint Commonwealth effort, was to book their ticket for another day.

In Australia, which at that time had no crews experienced in sailing international racing yachts greater than 8 Metres, there had been a boom in sailing, and several big spenders had been toying with the idea of building a contender for the Cup. Of these Sir Frank Packer, who had made a fortune from publishing, was the first afloat with *Gretel*, drawn by Alan Payne, then Australia's only full-time naval architect, with the aid of *Vim*, Vanderbilt's former 12 Metre, which he had chartered. It was a shrewd move, for not only did the Australians have the second fastest Twelve in America to tune up with, but as a result Payne was able to test scale models based on her lines at the Stevens Institute of Technology in America. Although the New York Yacht Club had just stated categorically that the 1962 challenger must be designed and built in Australia, Payne had already bent the rules, and even *Gretel*'s sails, numbering over eighty, were cut from American Dacron. Indeed, Payne went one step further by linking two American 'coffee grinders', as the jib-sheet winches were now called, through a single clutch mechanism, so that four men, instead of the usual two, could apply their muscle-power, thus giving the yacht a significant advantage.

It was possible that the New York Yacht Club, by allowing the challenger such leeway, were trying to avoid a repeat performance of 1958, but when they heard reports of *Gretel*'s excellent showing in Australia, they agreed that such generosity had to come to an end. Three older boats were already available to them, *Columbia*, *Easterner* and *Weatherly*, but because of general complacency, only one new Twelve, *Nefertiti*, commissioned by a Boston syndicate, had been considered necessary. It was almost a decision they lived to regret.

There followed some of the most exacting trials Americans had ever seen. Although *Easterner*, sailed more for fun as a family venture, was soon discarded, there was little to choose between the remaining yachts, and it was only because of Emil S. Mosbacher's determination at the helm of *Weatherly* that she was finally chosen to defend. 'Bus', as he was affectionately called, knew what was required of a skipper by the New York Yacht Club selection committee, and it was not just a pretty face!

Jock Sturrock, who had prepared *Gretel* almost as well, was unfortunately not chosen to be her helmsman until the day before the race, and Packer, who liked to be in charge, made other last minute changes that did not help. 'His bluster and brass', wrote an observer, 'was a stalking horse for a mind as devious and sly as a barrel of snakes.'

The Cup races began on 15 September, watched by a large crowd including President Kennedy, also from a destroyer. *Gretel*'s inexperienced navigator, appointed by Packer that morning, soon made an error that cost *Gretel* two minutes on the wrong tack, and when a broken backstay lost her further valuable seconds, she was unable to make up the deficit and finished nearly four minutes adrift. It seemed to prove very little, but the canny Mosbacher already knew that the Aussies had built the faster boat.

The second race, held three days later over the triangular course in a twenty-knot wind, turned swiftly into a tacking duel. Mosbacher, slightly ahead at the start, desperately tried to cover Sturrock, who was gaining with *Gretel*'s superior winches on every turn, but as the spray flew and the two boats were slammed from tack to tack, he wisely disengaged before it was too late. Leading after the first leg by a slender twelve seconds, he gained two more seconds on the next 8-mile reach, but on gybing *Weatherly* round the final mark he had a problem with his spinnaker, and before it had filled *Gretel* was on them with a war cry which could be heard for miles.

Lifted by a rogue wave, perhaps caused by some wandering Atlantic swell, *Gretel* nosed over the crest and plunged forward like a surfer at Bondi, with a crewman standing at her mast hollering his lungs out. She surged on and on, with her wake smoking in the sunlight, and taking *Weatherly*'s wind as she careered past, she won by nearly half a minute, beating the course record.

Australia went mad, and so large was the crowd of reporters in Newport when she was berthed, that they almost capsized the pontoon. 'GRETEL THE GREAT' were the headlines, 'One all, and everything to play for.' It was a fine win, but sadly it could not quite be repeated. Although the third race was an anticlimax, the fourth was again a crowd stopper. Tricked by Mosbacher close to the finish, much as Sherman Hoyt had robbed Sopwith of certain victory in 1934, Sturrock failed to press home his attack, and lost by the narrowest margin in the Cup's history.

The fifth race, won narrowly again by Mosbacher, finally dashed Australian hopes. But the series had shown just how surely a resolute country, with no previous experience of 12 Metres, could claim and one day would claim, the America's Cup.

In a welter of white water, *Gretel* surfs past *Weatherly* in a matter of seconds, riding high on a surging Atlantic roller

Gretel   Weatherly

1964 CONSTELLATION defeats SOVEREIGN

Constellation LOA: 65ft 5in
New York LWL: 45ft 1in
Yacht Club beam: 11ft 11in
draft: 8ft 11in
displacement: 58,411lbs (29 tons)
sail area: 1818sq ft

Owner: Walter Gubelman and syndicate
Designer: Sparkmann & Stephens
Builder: Minneford
Skipper: Robert Bavier and Eric Ridder

Sovereign LOA: 69ft
Royal LWL: 45ft 9in
Thames beam: 12ft 7in
draft: 8ft 11in
displacement: 62,000lbs (31 tons)
sail area: 1860sq ft

Owner: J. A. J. Boyden
Designer: David Boyd
Builder: Alex Robertson & Sons
Skipper: Peter Scott

If the British challenge in 1958 was a disappointment, the challenge of 1964 could only be described as a disaster.

After the close *Weatherly* and *Gretel* match of 1962, the British, having been baulked by the Aussies, and whose interest in the America's Cup had surprisingly increased as a result of *Sceptre*'s annihilation four years earlier, were determined to have another go in 1963. Overtures were made to the New York Yacht Club in vain, however, for the club had no intention of financing a defender again so quickly, or of asking crews to become entirely professional. Instead they agreed to a British challenge for 1964, and fixed that future matches would take place only once every three years.

Tony Boyden, a British self-made tycoon, having bought Hugh Goodsons's 12 Metre *Flica II*, had been working up a challenge for some time, and he was quite happy to accept David Boyd's design for a new boat, to be launched in 1963, believing that Boyd had learned a lot from his mistakes with *Sceptre*. Boyd had indeed tested his latest models at the Stevens Institute in America, but only just in the nick of time. *Gretel*, in 1962, had benefitted so much from American technology that the New York Yacht Club decreed that in future all challengers would have to be designed, tested and fitted out in their mother countries, and they made it clear that the Institute was no longer available.

Boyd had high hopes for his somewhat conventional brain-child, and *Sovereign* was duly launched at Alexander Robertsons, where *Sceptre* had been built, in June 1963. However Frank Packer, playing the Australian tough guy, thought differently, and his attempt to pit her against *Gretel* in an elimination race had to be quickly brushed off by the Royal Thames Yacht Club, who wanted to keep the challenge to themselves. At last, it seemed to them, the challenger would have a decent amount of time for working up, but after a few skirmishes with *Sceptre*, who beat her several times, there remained a certain nagging doubt about her qualifications to fight at all.

The British felt that somehow a back-up contender would have to be found, but it was not until August that two Australians, Frank and John Livingston, stepped forward to fill the breach. Unfortunately their offer came just too late, and because no yard would guarantee delivery of a new design, instead the brothers had to accept second best by getting Robertsons to build a sister-ship to *Sovereign*, later christened *Kurrewa V*. It was, perhaps, a little unimaginative to buy yet another horse from the same stable, particularly when the blood-lines were entirely suspect!

Two new boats had been commissioned in America, *Constellation* by a syndicate headed by Walter Gubelmann, heir to an office machine fortune, and *American Eagle* by a syndicate under Pierre S. duPont of the chemical family; and two older yachts, *Nefertiti* and the 1958 defender *Columbia*, had been refitted solely for the match. But as a result of the preliminary trials, which started in June 1964, *American Eagle* and *Constellation* were soon left to fight it out. 'Beat the Bird' read the stickers, as *American Eagle* started winning, but then, when Bob Bavier took the helm of *Constellation*, the tide began to turn and the 'Bird's' supporters were throwing rolls of lavatory paper stamped with 'prevent constipation'. It sounded like fun, but the trials had been held in deadly earnest, and for the first time in America helmsmen were getting the sack if they did not produce winning form. In the final leg of the race in which, as Bavier commented, they 'broke the *Eagle*'s heart', Bavier tacked *Constellation* no less than forty times, setting a record, and she went on to win selection by a whisker.

Initially the two British contenders, *Sovereign* and *Kurrewa V*, appeared to be almost as evenly matched, but when the races were resumed off Newport *Sovereign* began to inch ahead. This was the first time that two challengers under different ownership had continued their elimination trials in America, and for once long-term planning seemed to be paying off. It was also fortunate that Owen Aisher, managing *Kurrewa V*, had agreed to hand over all her sails to *Sovereign*, should she lose, and when she did, *Sovereign* was able to improve her inadequate wardrobe. Not that *Kurrewa*'s sails were anything to write home about, for her speed in England had probably been due to her American Dacron sails, and they, as a result of the new rules, had all been discarded.

Peter Scott, son of Scott of the Antarctic, *Sovereign*'s skipper, had been working hard at licking his crew into shape, but they were not seamen and they had been selected, more for their beef, from a group of rugger players. Scott, a noted explorer, painter, author and naturalist, was an accomplished glider pilot and dinghy helmsman, but his experience of offshore racing was limited, and later his appointment was criticised.

The first Cup race was held on 15 September. Both boats had a good start and in fluky conditions *Constellation* came home an inconclusive winner by five and a half minutes. But, after one day's postponement, the second race was held in a cleaner wind blowing at twenty knots from the south, and this was expected to favour *Sovereign*. Scott again achieved an excellent start, but as *Sovereign* drove into the long swell left by a passing hurricane, the story of *Sceptre* began to repeat itself. Rocking horse, or hobby horse, but certainly not a racehorse, *Sovereign* suffered from the same design faults as her sister, and as *Constellation* knifed away to weather, Scott was left helpless. He probably wished he could have retired gracefully then, but the America's Cup is not so forgiving. Losing by over twenty minutes, the largest margin since 1886, he was forced to endure two more defeats before it was finally all over.

At least Scott had won the starts, but the superior design of the defender, drawn by Olin Stephens to incorporate the best of the Twelves, *Vim* and *Columbia*, and *Constellation*'s better sails and more experienced crew, were unbeatable.

Constellation knifes away to weather as *Sovereign* ships it green. In the background the *Joseph P. Kennedy* stands guard

shipping it green

Constellation   Briggs Cunningham   *Sovereign*   Peter Scott

1967 INTREPID defeats DAME PATTIE

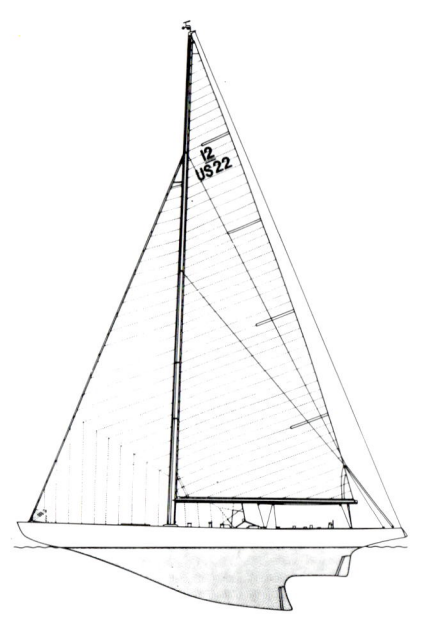

Intrepid	LOA: 64ft	Owner:
New York	LWL: 45ft 6in	Intrepid syndicate
Yacht Club	beam: 12ft	Designer:
	draft: 9ft	Sparkman & Stephens
	displacement: 57,500lbs	Builder:
	(29 tons)	Minneford
	sail area: 1850sq ft	Skipper: Bus Mosbacher

Dame Pattie	LOA: 65ft 2in	Owner:
Royal	LWL: 46ft 11in	Emil Christensen and
Sydney	beam: 11ft 11in	syndicate of commercial
Yacht	draft: 9ft 1in	firms
Squadron	displacement: 58,000lbs	Designer: Warwick Hood
	(29 tons)	Builder: William Barnett
	sail area: 1795sq ft	Skipper: Jock Sturrock

The Australians were lit up by their close encounter with *Gretel* in 1962, and two challenges, one by Sir Frank Packer and the other by an Australian businessman, Emil Christensen, were posted off to New York almost before the Americans had managed to uncork the champagne.

The revised rules, stating that in future all new boats and equipment had to be home manufactured, were of no consequence to Packer, who declaring that he was going to do some minor repairs to *Gretel*, cunningly got Alan Payne to completely rebuild her below the water-line, and then refitted all the old equipment and sails he had acquired in America for the 1962 match. For Christensen life was not so simple and, unlike Packer in 1962, he had to start from scratch. At least he was able to commission Warwick Hood, Payne's capable assistant, to design his new boat, but there were plenty of other problems, such as finding sails, which to many would have seemed insuperable.

The Australian elimination races, although demonstrating that *Gretel* was much improved, were won easily by Christensen's *Dame Pattie*. Named after the wife of Australia's former Prime Minister, Sir Robert Menzies, 'The Dame' had been built with a long water-line but with a short keel in order to reduce wetted surface, and weight had been saved by blunting her bow. Jock Sturrock, chosen as her skipper, knew that she was nothing sensational, and when she arrived to tune up against the chartered *Nefertiti* in Newport, and he got wind of the opposition, there began a war of words never before heard outside a boxing ring.

Psychological warfare was not new to the America's Cup, but the Aussies now had it worked out to a fine art. 'TWO MORE SECRETS FROM THE DAME' read the headlines from the *Sydney Sun* on 6 September, 'On the eve of the Cup, *Dame Pattie*'s crew are preparing two more deadly weapons.' The Americans had already been told of the others. First, there was a 'vortex generator' consisting of aluminium strips fastened to her 90ft (30m) mast, designed to force wind into her mainsail under certain conditions. Second, there was an electronic luffing indicator and, third, there was a box of tricks that worked out the distances sailed to windward on different legs. But that was not all. It was said that her rigging had been sheathed with revolving plastic aerofoils which would drive her along under bare poles, and that her sails were cut from a secret Australian material that was lighter than gossamer and stronger than sheet steel!

Bus Mosbacher, who had again been put in command of the defender, was not amused. He made no secret of the bad blood existing between the two teams at Newport, and told the press: 'If it's war they want, then it's war they'll get.' But some Americans were more worried: 'The Kangaroos don't appreciate how much we have got to lose', wrote one commentator. 'If we cannot defeat them with all our technological advantages and resources, it's time we gave our country back to the Indians.'

American concern was unfounded, for their *Intrepid* won eighteen of her nineteen trial races against *Columbia*, *Constellation* and *American Eagle*, and she was, as the Australians had already suspected, a killer. Bill Strawbridge and his syndicate had put tremendous effort into *Intrepid*'s design, and it was said that $45,000 had been spent on tank testing alone. She was not a pretty boat, because like 'The Dame', her stem, instead of following a graceful curve, was snipped sharply upwards in order to save weight and reduce pitching in a head sea. But Olin Stephens, designer of two previous America's Cup 12 Metre winners, had used every idea in the book to squeeze the most from the restrictive international rules, and *Intrepid* had features that the Australians had never dreamt of.

Stephens, copying one idea from *Enterprise*, the victor in 1930, first put all except the jib-sheet winches and their operators below decks. Then setting the rudder well back under her 'bustle', her rounded drag-efficient stern section, he added a trim tab to her stumpy keel, controlled by levers from the helm. But more importantly, by clearing the deck, he was able to reduce the height of her boom, resulting in better performance from the mainsail. This was kept a closely-guarded secret, and when *Intrepid* was inspected by the Aussies Stephens juggled with the winches and successfully held their attention away from these more vital statistics, for she was the most radical 12 Metre yet built.

Against such a boat *Dame Pattie* and her tough skipper, dubbed the 'Queensland Crocodile', stood no chance. 'Beaten all the way', shouted the media, and the only time *Intrepid* was in trouble was in the blustery third race when she had to avoid a coastguard helicopter, busy rescuing the crew of a sailing dinghy which had been capsized by its down-draught directly in her path.

The Australians were not downhearted and, saying that they felt better for the experience, they swore to return. They had been defeated by the combination of a great skipper, a well trained crew, better sail power and a boat which some elevated to the same pedestal as the mighty *Ranger*, winner in 1937.

Tossing spray, 'The Dame' is left behind by *Intrepid*, while in the background a rescue is taking place

capsized dinghy   rescue helicopter

Intrepid   *Dame Pattie*

1970 INTREPID defeats GRETEL II

Intrepid
New York Yacht Club

LOA: 64ft 6in
LWL: 47ft
beam: 12ft 3in
draft: 9ft 3in
displacement: 65,000lbs (32.5 tons)
sail area: 1750sq ft

Owner: Intrepid syndicate
Designer: Sparkman & Stephens
Builder: Minneford
Skipper: Bill Ficker

Gretel II
Royal Sydney Yacht Squadron

LOA: 62ft
LWL: 46ft
beam: 12ft 6in
draft: 9ft 6in
displacement: 63,000lbs (31.5 tons)
sail area: 1750sq ft

Owner: Sir Frank Packer
Designer: Alan Payne
Builder: William Barnett
Skipper: Jim Hardy

The America's Cup was to change course dramatically from 1970. No longer was it just a needle match between two determined clubs, it was fast becoming a major international event.

The 1967 contest had been watched eagerly by several future aspirants, and immediately it was over four different countries, England, Australia, France and Greece, sent in challenges within the required time limit of thirty days. Not unreasonably, the New York Yacht Club were reluctant to choose the challenger any more themselves, and so they appointed the Australians to run a series of selection trials off Newport, with the winner to be confirmed by an international jury.

One of the onlookers in 1967 had been the legendary Frenchman, Baron Bich, the Bic Biro magnate. Bich, who had nine children, decided one year to buy them a 12 Metre rather than pay for an expensive family holiday on the Riviera. The boat he set his heart on was *Kurrewa V*, built by the Livingston brothers in 1964 as a potential Cup challenger, and although hardly impressive in 1970 terms, she proved wonderful for picnics, and what was more, renamed *Levrier de Mers*, she gave Bich that sensational complaint, the 'Newport Bug'.

'Cup Fever', as it is otherwise known, is often nothing more serious than the desire to spend money. The Baron, however, suffered worse than many, and his illness developed rapidly into the form of four more 12 Metres! First he bought *Sovereign*, *Kurrewa*'s sister, soon followed by *Constellation*, which had defeated *Sovereign* in 1964; then he commissioned an American designer, Britton Chance Jr, to draw the lines of a new boat, *Chancegger*, which he had built by a Swiss named, naturally, Herr Egger. Needless to say none of these yachts had originated in his mother country, which still had no 12 Metres, but they did give his personal designer, Andre Mauric, plenty of food for thought, and by combining ideas used by Stephens in 1967 on *Intrepid*, he was able to put together a creditable performer named *France*.

The Aussies, before setting off for Newport with *Gretel II*, their new Alan Payne design, had wondered, on hearing that the British and Greeks had dropped out, what the French would have to offer, but even they were mildly surprised when the Baron arrived complete with three 12 Metres, several support ships, sixty sailors, two chefs and gallons of French wine!

Gretel failed to get her final rig from her designer until the eleventh hour, but despite this and the fact that *France* had been re-equipped with twenty-seven mainsails and fifteen spinnakers, each carrying the emblem of a French province, she won her first four races. Then, in the deciding event, which perhaps should not have been run at all, the unfortunate Baron, who had taken over the helm himself, got lost in the fog.

Meanwhile, a struggle was developing for the right to defend, made all the fiercer by a young and dynamic TV tycoon from Atlanta, Georgia. Ted Turner, the only man then to have won the famous Southern Ocean Racing Committee (SORC) trophy twice, was out to get the nomination at all costs, and it was much to the relief of the West Coast hierarchy when, on this occasion, he failed to complete his preparations in time. This meant that two new yachts, *Valiant* and *Heritage*, were left to fight it out with the veteran *Weatherly*, and *Intrepid*, now helmed by Bill Ficker. Ficker won through, generously providing Americans with a fresh slogan, 'Ficker is Quicker'.

Sir Frank Packer, *Gretel*'s wily owner, opened the batting for the big match by objecting to the fairings fitted to *Intrepid*'s rudder and the lack of screening around her 'heads', which, against the rules, gave no privacy to those with time to visit them. But the modifications made little difference, and *Intrepid*'s crew did have time, but only just.

In the first race it was *Gretel* that got into trouble, and when her spinnaker pole was broken because of a tangled sail, and her foredeck chief fell overboard, she was already beaten. The second race, having been postponed because of fog, was a cliff-hanger. Tension was already running high, and when at the start Ficker tried to squeeze between Martin Visser, driving *Gretel*, and the committee boat, the Aussies wouldn't have it; there was a collision, and protest flags were hoisted everywhere. *Gretel*, although losing her false bow, and slower away, went on to win with Jim Hardy at the helm, but only to be disqualified for 'barging at the start', the very crime of which she was accusing her rival. Packer swore that he would get a ruling from the Supreme Court, and the foul eventually created almost as much steam as 'The Luffing Incident' had in 1934.

It was not all over, however, and the Aussies, swallowing their indignation, shared the next two races. But in the final contest Ficker took the honours by less than two minutes, making it one of the closest series ever held for the America's Cup.

Gretel II lost the protest because the committee concluded that 'at the start she had sailed above the wind', a decision that the Australians contested. (The incident was painted with help from an aerial photograph, shown in the introduction to this book.)

Intrepid   *Gretel II*   committee boat

1974 COURAGEOUS defeats SOUTHERN CROSS

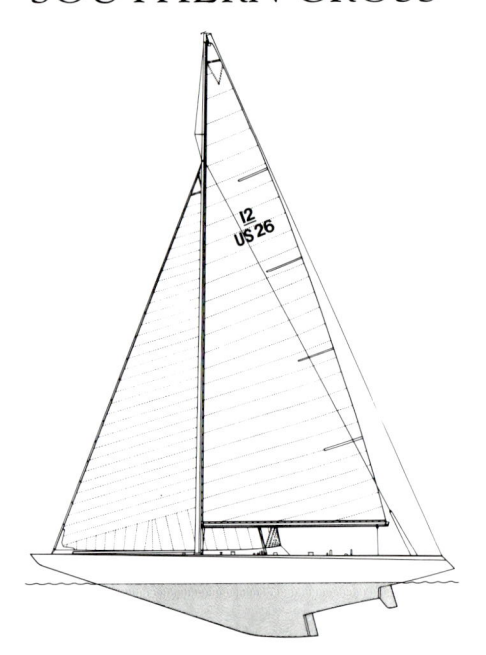

Courageous
New York
Yacht Club

LOA: 66ft
LWL: 45ft
beam: 12ft
draft: 8ft 10in
displacement: 58,000lbs
(29 tons)
sail area: 1770sq ft

Owner:
Courageous syndicate
Designer:
Sparkman & Stephens
Builder:
Minneford
Skipper: Robert Bavier

Southern Cross
Royal Perth

LOA: 67ft 3in
LWL: 46ft 8in
beam: 12ft 4in
draft: 9ft 6in
displacement: 62,000lbs
(31 tons)
sail area: 1811sq ft

Owner:
Alan Bond
Designer: Bob Miller
Builder:
Halvorsen, Morson & Gowland
Skipper: John Cuneo

The twenty-second challenge for the America's Cup, which should have taken place in 1973, is remembered not so much for its somewhat predictable conclusion but more for its unusual start. The defenders may well have looked down a gun barrel before, but this time it was from the wrong end!

In 1970 the New York Yacht Club had extended the period for submitting challenges from thirty to ninety days, and during this period eight aspiring clubs from Great Britain, Australia, Canada, France and Italy had sent in their applications. But although this was a pointer for the future, only the French, headed by the now legendary Baron Bich, and the Australians, with a new man Alan Bond in the hot seat, ultimately got their campaigns off the ground.

Bond, who, since leaving London at the age of thirteen, had amassed a fortune from real estate in Western Australia, was not slow to declare war; and making no pretence of his distaste for the methods of the New York Yacht Club race committee, he warned them that he would be taking his lawyer to Newport along with a videotape camera crew instructed to get everything on record. It was to be the start of the most pugnacious and protracted onslaught on the Cup in its entire history.

The Baron, however, was in trouble right from the outset. Although by now the French had learned a great deal about the game and were certainly a force to be reckoned with, Bich overstepped the mark by employing a Dane to co-ordinate his latest offensive. Paul Elvstrom was one of the most distinguished helmsmen in the world, and had won four Olympic gold medals for sailing, but that meant very little to the Baron's compatriots who, supicious that Elvstrom was about to employ a Scandinavian crew, or even build his own boat, were looking for every excuse to have him ousted. They were not to be frustrated for very long. The 'Great Dane', as he was soon named, made his first mistake when *France* sank in a gale while being towed back from the Baltic, and he then compounded his problems by being beaten by Frenchmen in the 1972 Olympics and the 1973 Half-ton World Championships. Needless to say the French had been more intent on having the wretched Elvstrom's head than collecting the trophies, and when the French press also joined in the sport the Baron had no alternative but to send him his marching orders.

The Baron might well have given up then and there, but instead he stopped any further work being done on the new yacht he was building and, thinking ahead, sent the salvaged *France* to Newport in the capable hands of Jean-Marie Le Guillou, who later may have wished he had stayed at home.

Bond had spared nothing. Having bought both *Gretel* and *Gretel II*, he had a vast concrete hangar constructed for them and his new Bob Miller designed *Southern Cross* at his Yanchep Sun City, which he had festooned with barbed wire and patrolled by dogs. Space-age technology had arrived, and as far as Bond was concerned the developments in aluminium hull construction (allowed by the rules since 1970) kevlar sails and on-board computers, were too important to be shared with anyone.

The Americans, aware of what was going on, were preparing for the defence with more than their usual thoroughness, but there was a sense of relief when the match, owing to the deepening international recession, which may have gone unnoticed by Bich and Bond, was postponed for a year until 1974. The *Courageous* syndicate actually ran out of funds at one stage and lost Bill Ficker, their proposed helmsman, before William Strawbridge was persuaded by the New York Yacht Club to continue with the yacht's construction and sign Bob Bavier, the 1964 winning captain, instead. *Mariner* was not so affected, however, because George Hinman, her manager, developed a tax-exempt scheme in order to raise the one million dollars required – but she was not so clever on the water, and it was unfortunate that Hinman found it necessary to replace Ted Turner, her experienced ocean racing skipper, with Dennis Conner, before she finally failed and was withdrawn. Turner did not go much on *Mariner*'s design, or for that matter on her designer either, and when *Valiant*, Britton Chance's other similar boat, was also thrashed by both *Courageous* and the fierce old *Intrepid*, he was proved right. *Intrepid* lost the final selection trials only in the last of nine hard-fought races, and *Courageous* could have found no better sparring partner.

Courageous, skippered by Ted Hood, was an Olin Stephens classic. Lighter and smaller than many 12 Metres, she was also some six inches too long, a fact only discovered before her subsequent defence of the Cup in 1977, when she was altered accordingly.

Southern Cross was also an unusual boat, similarly built with long overhangs designed to increase her speed on the wind. But she had some difficulty shaking off *Gretel II*, and it was only when Jim Hardy was transferred to her helm from that of the older yacht that the mustard-yellow ('Yanchep'-yellow) lady picked up her skirts, trouncing *France* 4–0 in the elimination series.

The Cup races, after all this excitement, were very disappointing and *The Cross* never came up to expectations. Conner, who had moved to *Courageous* as her tactician and starting helmsman, was not so sure, however, and only his clever use of wind shifts in the first two races got *Courageous* into the lead. In the second race *The Cross* managed to hold on remarkably well, losing out to her opponent only by putting in more tacks, and on the second leg, which was a run, she made up half the lost ground. But although later the frustrated Bond made various crew changes and did some splendid 'coffee grinding' himself, it was only to be counter-productive and after plenty of protests and counter-protests *Courageous* finished with a clean sweep.

Ian Dear, writing in his *Informal History of the America's Cup*, states that when Hardy was asked how he slept after losing the first race he said: 'Like a baby. I woke up every two hours and cried.' Perhaps there were many such nights for the Australians still to come!

Downwind in the second race, *Courageous* set her red, white and blue North spinnaker, a gift from the *Mariner* syndicate, while *Southern Cross*, flying her magnificent white spinnaker, made up almost thirty seconds to the wing mark

winner 1974 and 1977

Courageous   Southern Cross

1977 COURAGEOUS defeats AUSTRALIA

Courageous New York Yacht Club	LOA: 66ft LWL: 44ft 6in beam: 12ft draft: 8ft 10in displacement: 56,000lbs (28 tons) sail area: 1770sq ft	Owner: Kings Point Fund Inc Designer: Sparkman & Stephens Builder: Minneford Skipper: Ted Turner

Australia Sun City	LOA: 64ft 6in LWL: 47ft beam: 12ft 3in draft: 9ft 1in displacement: 58,000lbs (29 tons) sail area: 1800sq ft	Owner: Alan Bond Designer: Bob Miller and Johan Valentijn Builder: William Barnett Skipper: Noel Robins

The America's Cup of 1974 had incited two of the combatants to continue with campaigns which were to rank amongst the most ruthless ever fought over water.

Alan Bond, who in 1976 for once was not feeling flush with money, had at first indicated that he was pulling out, but underneath his brash exterior he was made of sterner stuff. Having patched up some differences with Bob Miller (who later changed his name to Ben Lexcen), he asked him to design a new and lighter 12 Metre, more suitable to the fluky conditions off Newport than *Southern Cross* had been, and as a result announced the birth of *Australia*.

Ted Turner, still smarting from his replacement during 1974 as *Mariner*'s skipper, was also holding on to his small beginnings in the Cup like a terrier, and nothing was going to prevent him from having another go. For some time Turner had been coveting *Courageous*, for he was determined to buy himself a yacht which had already excelled at the game, and his fury was understandable when A. Lee Loomis, an ardent member of the New York Yacht Club, from which the flamboyant Turner had twice been refused membership, acquired *Courageous* for the Hood syndicate under his very nose.

For Turner, however, there were no other fish in the sea, so waving a fistful of dollars he set about persuading the 'Big Loom', as he disrespectfully called Loomis, to sell him the helm instead. Loomis, he later discovered, was not worried. *Courageous* had been acquired only as a trial horse for a new Hood design to be called *Independence*, which was to be skippered by the great Ted Hood himself.

Commercialism was already starting to taint the sporting nature of the Cup, and when *Enterprise*, a new American Twelve skippered by Lowell North, took the stage, a futile but bitter rivalry developed between the world's leading sail makers, which was to last throughout the summer. Turner had himself tried to equip *Courageous* with North sails, a company he had always supported, and when he failed, believing it was due to his connection with Hood, he swore that he would work against North for the rest of his life.

Meanwhile, outside the battle zone, the prospective challengers had their own problems. Baron Bich, as determined as ever, had commissioned a new boat, *France II*, but when she was unable to beat *France I* he was forced to alter the older yacht to comply with the new New York Yacht Club rules. In line with ocean racing practice, the rules stated that in future all winches would have to be on deck, open hatches would be limited, and self-draining cockpits made compulsory. It meant that for a crucial summer month *France I* had to be out of the water, and partly as a result she never became competitive.

For the first time Sweden had also entered the fray. Launched by Queen Sylvia, *Sverige* was the first yacht to have been wholly financed by a nation's industry, and surprisingly she had been fitted with, instead of two wheels, an old-fashioned tiller. It was to prove very effective, particularly at the starts, and she went on to beat *Gretel II*, whose crew of forty-year-olds were known as 'Dad's Navy', in the elimination series, only to be thrashed convincingly by *Australia* in the finals.

During the previous winter *Courageous* had also been slipped for modifications, and when it was discovered that she had been measured wrongly in 1974, she was given a complete facelift. With this under his belt, and now guaranteed the helm, Turner was sure that he could knock spots off Hood, so he set about doing so, cheered on by his Atlanta Braves baseball team. Only two more obstacles still remained: one was George Hinman, who had sacked him as *Mariner*'s skipper, and who was now unfortunately chairman of the Cup selection committee, and the other was *Enterprise*. Turner tackled them both with a cool head and won through.

For Turner it was a great personal triumph. It was unheard of for a sacked skipper to come back and be chosen to represent America, but he had done it, and such was his competitiveness that he had no intention in the races to follow of allowing *Australia* even a sniff at victory. He knew only too well that the odds were shortening on every challenge, and should America one day lose the Cup it was not going to be him that lost it.

The first of the best of seven races was held on 13 September, witnessed by a vast flotilla of naval ships, motor yachts, launches, sailing boats and other vessels, while silhouetted on the horizon could be seen the replica of the Revolutionary War sloop *Providence*, and the topsail schooner *Shenandoah*. As the contestants circled, like fighting cocks looking for an opening, Turner locked on to *Australia*'s stern endeavouring to push Noel Robins, her skipper, over the line early. Then, just as suddenly, he broke away and, starting several seconds late but on the more favourable tack, he snatched a lead that he never relinquished.

The second race, sailed in wet conditions under a glowering sky, was no different; *Courageous* was already two minutes ahead at the weather mark, and only on the run did *Australia* make any impression on her. It was her only chance, for Turner quickly closed the door and then covered so well for the rest of the series that Robins was soundly defeated.

When *Courageous* docked after the deciding race, the crowd went mad, and Turner, his crew, and several members of the committee were flung into the drink. But the unpopular 'Loom', who had bravely continued to manage the defence despite his scorn for Turner, was left to leap in all on his own.

Courageous sets her spinnaker and heads off downwind in the second race

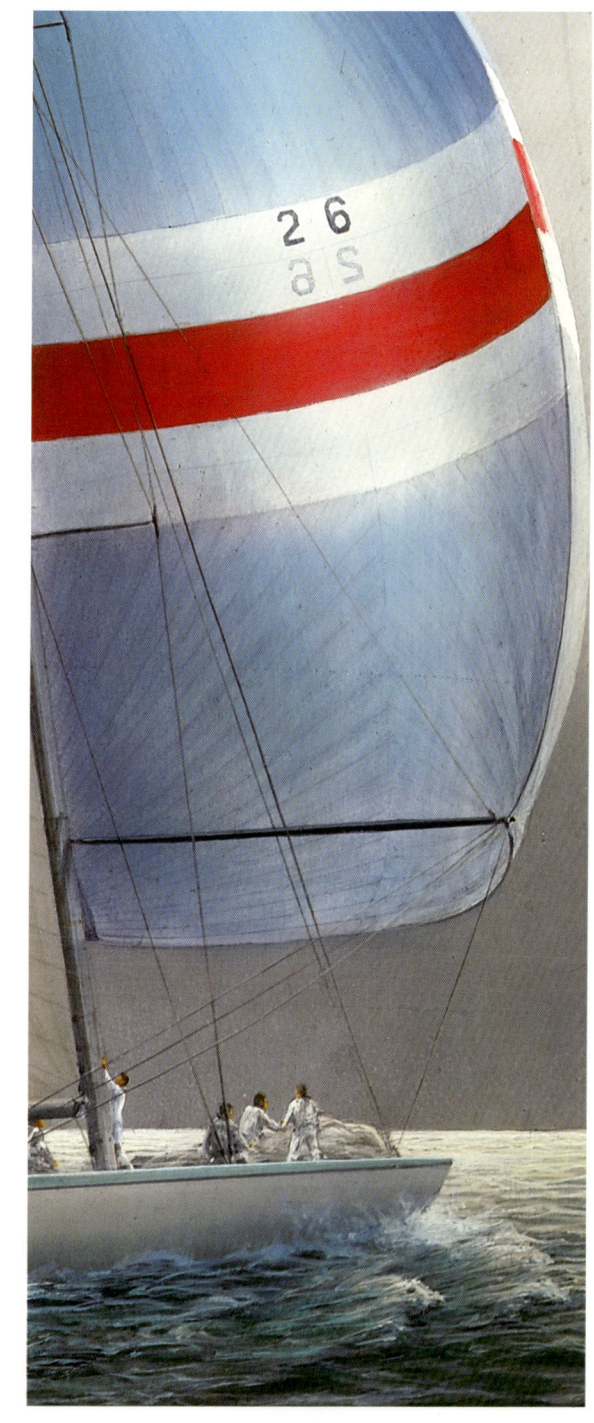

up spinnaker

Australia   Courageous

1980
FREEDOM defeats AUSTRALIA

Freedom	LOA: 63ft	Owner:
New York	LWL: 47ft	Fort Schuyler Foundation
Yacht Club	beam: 12ft	*Designer*
	draft: 9ft	Sparkmann & Stephens
	displacement: 61,000lbs	*Builder:* Minneford
	(30.5 tons)	*Skipper:* Dennis Conner
	sail area: 1800sq ft	

Australia	LOA: 64ft 6in	Owner: Alan Bond
Royal	LWL: 47ft	*Designer:*
Perth	beam: 12ft 3in	Ben Lexcen and
	draft: 9ft 1in	Johan Valentijn
	displacement: 58,000lbs	*Builder:*
	(29 tons)	William Barnett
	sail area: 1800sq ft	*Skipper:* Jim Hardy

Australia's five challenges for the America's Cup had given yachting a tremendous boost 'down under' and, despite Bond's crushing defeat in 1977 at the hands of Ted Turner, they were back for further punishment in 1980 with a much revamped *Australia*.

Baron Bich, refreshed after his débâcle over Elvstrom, was also back in his immaculate white linen uniform complete with white gloves and yachting cap, accompanied this time by *France III*, and Pelle Petterson had returned with a greatly modified *Sverige*. But perhaps the most dramatic entry was that of the British, who after sixteen years absence from the Cup scene, produced *Lionheart*, the yacht with a banana mast. Hooked back several feet at the tip, it had been designed to give her more sail area on top and 10 per cent more unmeasured sail overall, and it immediately set the tongues wagging, particularly amongst the Australians. Ben Lexcen, *Australia*'s designer, who had spent a fortnight pondering over *Lionheart*'s bent stick, eventually came to the conclusion: 'I'd been thinking that the mast was somehow British property and that we couldn't touch it. Then it occurred to me that if we had their mast we could win the bloody Cup!'

As the challengers' trails got under way the Australians were playing it cool, but only two doors away from the American camp, in an old unlocked shed but in utmost secrecy, a small team were hard at it fashioning a new stick for their boat, based on the hundreds of photographs they had blatantly taken of *Lionheart*. The British yacht, as expected, definitely had the edge in light airs, and they were certain that by stepping an improved version of her mast on *Australia*'s superior hull they would have a winner. Poor *Lionheart*, in the stronger winds she did not perform so well, and with *Sverige*, which had also failed to come up to expectations, she was eliminated in the first of the round-robin series, won by *Australia* 6–3.

In the final trials, and much to everyone's satisfaction, *France III*, with Bruno Trouble at the helm, managed to beat *Australia* in one of the four races, giving the resolute Baron at least some consolation for his years of trying.

The Americans had three boats to choose from: *Courageous*, which, having been bought by Ted Turner, seemed to have become the doyen of all 12 Metres; *Freedom*, a new boat sponsored through the tax-exempt Fort Schuyler Foundation, designed again by the great Olin Stephens; and *Clipper*, which was supported by Pan American Airways and which had been stitched together by David Pedrick from the cannibalised *Independence*. Turner was busy with his new satellite-transmitted television news service, and his 1977 form seemed to have left him, but Dennis Conner, who at the time was probably the most accomplished helmsman in the world, and who had been invited to sail *Freedom*, reigned supreme. Neither Turner nor Russell Long on *Clipper* got much of a look in, Conner winning thirty-seven of his forty races.

Needless to say, when the Australians turned out for the Cup on 16 September the supremo was furious. The winds for the series were expected to be on the light side, and when he first caught sight of *Australia*'s bendy mast he realised that they had as good as stolen the Cup from under his nose. Conner had thought of trying the idea himself, but had been too slow off the mark. Bond, applying the needle after the first race, which *Freedom* won, had *Australia*'s mast illuminated by floodlights all night long.

The second race ran over the time limit just as the Australians were about to stow it away in their tucker bag, but when it was rerun it was evident that their war of nerves was beginning to pay off. *Freedom*'s skipper was visibly rattled but, unknown to Jim Hardy on *Australia*, Conner, as was admitted later by one of his faithful crew, had already prepared a mischievous plan.

The match was being held late in the year, and as the winds were light Conner had calculated that at least one race would end as the sun went down. He had therefore asked his crew to check *Freedom*'s running lights and to keep them dry, ready to be brought on deck. *Australia* took the lead for the first four legs of the postponed second race, was momentarily overhauled by *Freedom* on the run, and then ghosted past her again with only minutes to go before they were obliged to finish. Against the sunset, and shadowed by a coastguard vessel, Hardy noticed the Americans fixing their lights, but when he tried to do likewise and failed, Conner ran up a protest flag as the Aussies went on to take the race.

It had been the first win by an Australian boat since Hardy had been denied the privilege when leading over the line with *Gretel II* in 1970, and in no way was Bond, calling for his lawyers, going to be cheated of victory again. But for the international jury that gathered that night to hear Conner put his case, the protest was clear: contrary to the rules, and also to maritime regulations, *Australia* had failed to display her running lights at sundown.

Bond countered that the rules only stated that yachts had to carry lights, not show them. When that did not wash, he explained that *Australia*'s stern light, a torch, had unfortunately been found out of action in the bilges, and that the deck-hand (gorilla) sent forrard to attach the bow lights had mistakenly hooked up port for starboard. The jury were sympathetic but not impressed, and only at the twelfth hour was the matter dropped when a somewhat bashful Conner failed to turn up for the final hearing.

It had been a futile incident, but in the end it was the mast and not Conner that had the last laugh. So secretive had the Aussies been about it before the first race that there had been no time to refashion their new kevlar-mylar mainsails correctly. Conner won the third race by a whisker, then in the fourth the Aussies put up the wrong sail, leaving themselves only one more chance. Sadly, on the last day the wind blew, and that did not suit their sails at all – but at least the Aussie's bent stick had softened up the enemy for 1983!

The Australians attempt to hook up their lights, but it is already too late

wrong light   no light

Australia   Freedom   coastguard

1983
AUSTRALIA II defeats LIBERTY

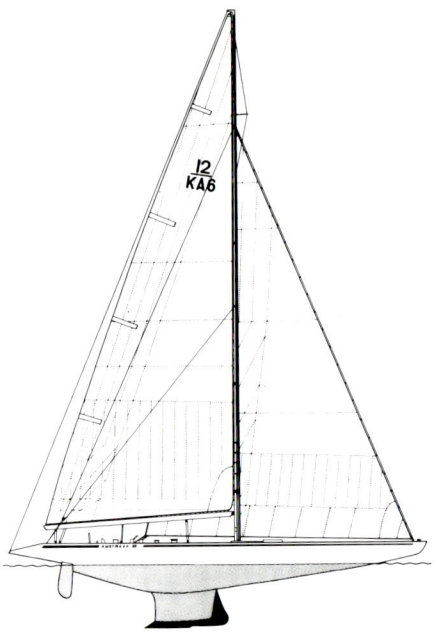

Australia II
Royal Perth
LOA: 64ft 7in
LWL: 44ft 2in
beam: 12ft
draft: 8ft 6in
displacement: 52,500lbs (26 tons)
sail area: 1820sq ft
Owner: Alan Bond
Designer: Ben Lexcen
Builder: Stephen Ward
Skipper: John Bertrand

Liberty
New York Yacht Club
LOA: 66ft
LWL: 45ft
beam: 12ft 3in
draft: 9ft 1in
displacement: 57,000lbs (approx) (28.5 tons)
sail area: 1825sq ft
Owner: Fort Schuyler Foundation
Designer: Johan Valentijn
Builder: Newport Offshore
Skipper: Dennis Conner

Australia's lead in the second race of 1980 before it was abandoned, and her one win, had really shaken Dennis Conner, but at least he felt happier when he learned that she had been sold, he believed mistakenly, to the British entrepreneur Peter de Savary.

De Savary, unlike most British challengers before him, set about his preparations in the most businesslike manner, and armed with three boats he started intensive evaluation trials first at home and then in America. These resulted in him building, to Ian Howlett's design, the subsequently much respected *Victory 83*, and it was with her, the transformed *Lionheart*, and a team of more than sixty people, that he arrived back in Newport during summer 1983 for a further period of rigorous training.

Equally determined challenges had been received from France, the young film producer Yves Rousset-Rouard taking on *France III* with the blessing of the illustrious Baron Bich; from Italy, with *Azzurra* which had been sponsored by a consortium of sixteen companies aided by Gianni Agnelli of Fiat and His Highness the Aga Khan; and from Canada, which had been absent from the America's Cup since *Atalanta* failed in 1881. After that wipe-out the New York Yacht Club had insisted that in future only an establishment fronting on the ocean would qualify, and so the Canadian syndicate had formed their own 'Secret Cove' Club, sixty miles north of Vancouver, borrowing two and a half million dollars to buy the 1980 contender *Clipper* and build their own creditable performer *Canada I*. But as the entrants were assembling for the final analysis, all eyes turned to the Australians, whose arrival with three yachts – *Challenge 12* from the State of Victoria; *Advance*, Syd Fischer's entry from New South Wales; and Alan Bond's *Australia II* from the Royal Perth Yacht Club – now made all previous Aussie attempts seem feeble.

Bond had spared no expense in sending his designer Ben Lexcen to evaluate one-third scale models at the tank-testing centre in Holland, causing the New York Yacht Club to protest that his boats were Dutch. It was only when he had completed this programme and had started playing with some extreme keel shapes that Lexcen found, much to his surprise, that one of them worked. The notorious winged keel had been born, and Lexcen was not slow to incorporate it in *Australia II*, his less radical design going to the Victorians as *Challenge 12*, thus providing Bond with an excellent yardstick.

The saga of the winged keel has already eclipsed all Cup stories that have gone before, but there is no doubt that from the moment *Australia II* arrived in Newport, the Americans knew that their number was up. The more elimination races she won, the more the New York Yacht Club tried to stop her, and her keel, shrouded under green polythene when she was hauled out, dominated their minds. At first it was Rule 7, 'if such peculiarities place the measurer in doubt', and then they found every other reason for making her keel illegal. Rarely had two 'friendly' competing nations been so much at each other's throats and Bond was the first to declare: 'This is not sport. It's war!'

By the time John Bertrand, driving *Australia II*, had overpowered *Victory 83* by 4–1 in the final trials, public opinion was firmly on the Aussies' side. Warren Jones, the boat's experienced executive director, had already unearthed a telex sent to the Dutch by an American syndicate manager asking for help in building the same keel that the New York Yacht Club were now desperately trying to ban. De Savary almost clinched it when he revealed that the keelboat committee had previously given his designer Howlett the go-ahead on a similar appendage. The writing was on the wall, and the race committee, faced by the alternative of cancelling the Cup, took the easy way out and avoided the vote.

Meanwhile the defence trials were held, with the old but rejuvenated *Courageous* making a fine start. *Defender*, skippered by Tom Blackaller, was however soon in trouble, and in an attempt to lift her ends a deep wedge was cut out of her middle – with a chainsaw. Alterations to *Liberty* were not so drastic and, with the somewhat apprehensive Dennis Conner at the helm, she improved all the time, finally dealing with the irrepressible *Courageous* and getting the nod.

The first Cup race was held on 13 September, but it was postponed due to fluky wind conditions. On the following day, in a good breeze, Conner took the initiative early on and won by over a minute. In the second race, started in similar conditions, *Liberty* did it again, this time overtaking *Australia II* on the second beat and winning by more than one and a half minutes. Then in the third contest, when all seemed lost, Bertrand pulled the rabbit out of the hat and crushed *Liberty* by over three minutes, the greatest margin by any challenger since 1871. It was a wonderful morale booster for the boys from 'down under', but their spirits were quickly doused when Conner took the fourth with a masterly display of helmsmanship. The fifth race had seemed a formality, but Bertrand again got it right, and in a stiffening breeze, he won by almost two minutes. It was the first time that the Cup had gone to six races since *Rainbow* had defeated *Endeavour* in 1934, and even those who could not tell a jib from a gybe, became captivated by the rapidly unfolding drama. They were not to be disappointed, for in the sixth race Conner failed to cover Bertrand on the first leg, allowing *Australia II* to snatch the lead and triumph by nearly three and a half minutes, levelling the score 3–3. The last act was about to be played, and the whole world waited to see if the Aussies could put an end to the Yankees' 132-year reign, the longest winning streak in sporting history.

The day dawned crisp and clear, and soon, as a gentle breeze arrived and the course signals were hoisted on *Black Knight*, the initial data began to be fed into the opponents' ravenous computers. Conner narrowly got the edge at the start, held it, and as the two boats approached the penultimate leg, millions of Australians, sitting glued to their television sets, groaned as *Liberty* romped on and into an almost unassailable one-minute lead. Then it happened. Bertrand, suddenly disengaging from *Liberty*'s stern, shot off to a darker patch of water, grabbed the wind and stormed past Conner before he had time to cover. Tack for tack Conner desperately tried to claw Bertrand back, but it was too late; after twenty-one years of valiant effort the Aussies were going for gold, and Bond was already cracking open a can of his Black Swan lager.

Conner stands powerless at the helm as America loses the Cup after a 132-year reign

Conner

Liberty   *Australia II*   committee boat (finishing line)

1987
STARS & STRIPES defeats KOOKABURRA III

Stars & Stripes
San Diego Yacht Club

LOA: 64ft 3in
LWL: 44ft 6in
beam: 12ft 6in
draft: 8ft 9in
displacement: 50,848lbs (22.7 tons)
sail area: 1540sq ft

Syndicate: Sail America
Chairman: Malin Burnham
Designers: Chance, Nelson, Pedrick
Skipper: Dennis Conner

Kookaburra III
Royal Perth Yacht Club

LOA: 67ft
LWL: 44ft
beam: 12ft 1in
draft: 9ft 1in
displacement: 54,880lbs (24.5 tons)
sail area: 1799sq ft

Syndicate: Taskforce 1987
Chairman: Kevin Parry
Designers: Murray, Swarbrick
Skipper: Iain Murray

On the night that *Australia II* won the cup in 1983, Alan Bond, in a wild moment he was later to regret, allowed her secret winged keel to be exposed to the press. It was the beginning of a technological scramble that has probably never been equalled, even in time of war.

Undaunted by the huge sums now required to put a competitive boat into the water, and attracted by the growing rewards to the vanquisher, fourteen challengers from Great Britain, the United States, France, Italy, Canada and New Zealand, set their sails for Perth. This new battleground, dominated by the notorious 'Fremantle Doctor', a fierce wind that blows inland from the Indian Ocean on a summer's afternoon to replace air rising from the hot Australian desert, demanded new standards of excellence; by the time racing began the total cost to all the syndicates competing was estimated to have risen to a staggering £150 million.

Alan Bond had already announced that this would be his last campaign, no win could measure up to 1983, and partly as a result of this, *Australia IV* never fully extended the best of the five other yachts built to defend the Cup. But in every other way the man had so determinedly wrested the trophy from the New York Yacht Club after so many years, had turned the event into a billion dollar bonanza. As the press gathered from twenty-six countries, and over fifty television networks started broadcasting the America's Cup throughout the world, his dreams began to come true.

The financial benefits for any club winning the Cup had become so great that as much time was spent on chasing up new sponsors as on the boats themselves. Individual budgets, at first set as low as £2 million, soon climbed to £8 million or more; the age of snap-on keels had arrived in earnest, and the maze of problems confronting designers trying to squeeze the last fraction of a knot out of their errant steeds, had become a financial nightmare.

Amongst those who did not sleep too well were the British *White Crusader* team, for the Royal Perth Yacht Club had stated that no new keels could be cast by the challengers on Australian soil. Flying £30,000 keels around the world at £70,000 a time becomes an expensive pastime, and harsh words were spoken with some effect. But the toughest words came from that old man of the sea, Dennis Conner, who with others was unhappy that the New Zealand team should race its innovative 'Plastic Fantastic' without having her first drilled full of inspection holes. No fibreglass boat had ever been raced in the America's Cup before, and by using this material it was possible to lighten her 'ends' to advantage. But his demands fell largely on deaf ears.

Dennis, the master of gamesmanship, had tuned up in Hawaii away from the fleet, unlike the rest of the challengers. Riding the big surf in Honolulu, he had found conditions very similar to those in Western Australia, and with the help of Boeing and NASA he had been able to develop his four boats in utmost secrecy. It was unfortunate that when his stable arrived off Fremantle one of his yachts got stuck on a 'bump', and had to be towed off by Bondy's boys, who must have had a quick peek. But he remained the dark horse just as he wanted to be, and as the round robin elimination series got under way in October 1986 and his gunsmoke-blue *Stars & Stripes* failed to shine, few could have realised that he was probably 'sandbagging'.

Horseracing stewards would not have looked kindly on *Stars & Stripes*'s jockey for not trying, but some may have given him the benefit of the doubt due to the lighter airs prevailing in the earlier rounds. Coming from behind he quietly notched up just enough wins to keep in touch, and then disposed of *French Kiss*, sponsored by Kis (a French company who were earlier accused of advertising), to meet the New Zealand boat in the finals of the challenger's series. Named *KZ7*, because 7 was the lucky number of her sponsor Michael Fay's string of racehorses, she had only once been defeated; when Dennis beat her convincingly, the New Zealand punters could have skinned him alive!

Iain Murray, well known for his prowess with the boisterous eighteen-footers in Sydney harbour, had won the defender series with the laughing *Kookaburra*, the golden hope of Kevin Parry, sporting more high-tech gear on deck than any yacht in history. But the black computer evaluation strips on her sails did not worry the *Stars & Stripes* camp at all. They had evaluated every yacht in Fremantle, using a Cray computer, the most powerful of its kind in the world; they knew that they had built a weapon that, in the stronger winds expected later on, would be some .02 knots faster than any other 12 Metre afloat.

It was thus that the finals of the 1987 match were, to many, an anticlimax. Only the 'Doctor' came fully up to expectations, making heroes of the intrepid bowmen and pale shadows of most of the contestants' ardent supporters.

Sailing faultlessly, and resorting to machiavellian mischief only twice, to introduce a 'Dolly Parton' spinnaker and a skin of tiny riblets to reduce drag, Dennis won the first race by 1 min 41 secs, and the second, after an exciting start, by a margin of 1 min 10 secs. The third race, won by 1 min 46, will be remembered for his epic 'duck' under the *Kookaburra*'s stern to snatch the lead on the initial beat. The fourth and final race, won by *Stars & Stripes* from the start by 1 min 59 secs, was therefore only a formality. Discarded as skipper by the New York Yacht Club, but sponsored by such notable organisations as the Ford Motor Company, Budweiser and Merrill Lynch, and flying his home San Diego colours, revenge had been very sweet. Dennis Conner, the first man to win back the America's Cup, counts only on excellence; but for those who may feel that he is now invincible, it is interesting to note that when he was later thrown into the dock, he couldn't swim!

Before the start of race 2, *Kookaburra III* chases *Stars & Stripes* round the spectator boat *Bengal I*, to try and get the dominant position. Iain Murray hoists a protest flag as Dennis Conner jibes across his bows to shut him out, but the protest fails

86

Stars & Stripes   Kookaburra III   Bengal I

1988
STARS & STRIPES defeats NEW ZEALAND

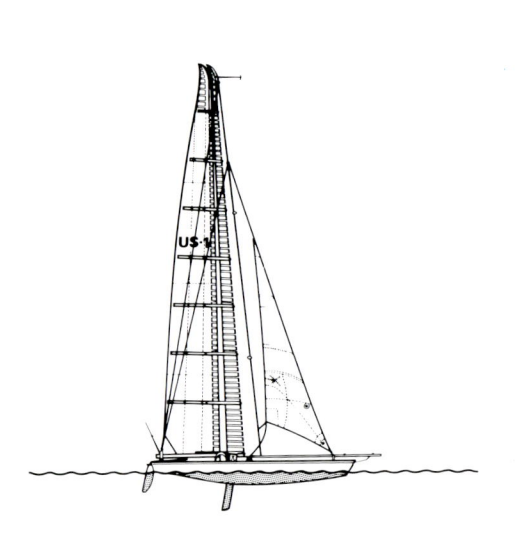

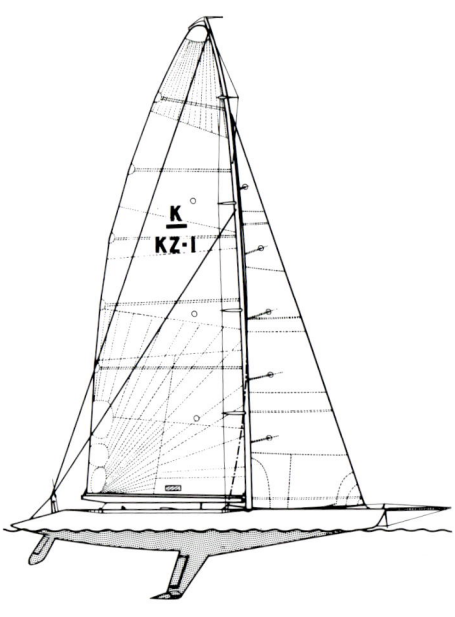

Stars & Stripes 1988 San Diego Yacht Club	LOA: 60ft 0in LWL: 55ft 0in beam: 30ft 0in draught: 10ft 1in displacement: 6,000lbs sail area: 1,900sq ft	Syndicate: Sail America Chairman: Malin Burnham Designers: Marshall, Chance Hubbard, Maclane, Morrelli, Nelson, Nivelt Skipper: Dennis Conner Crew: 8	New Zealand Mercury Bay Boating Club	LOA: 132ft 8in LWL: 90ft 0in beam: 26ft 0in draught: 21ft 0in displacement: 83,000lbs sail area: 7,500sq ft	Syndicate: Mercury Bay Chairman: Michael Fay Designers: Farr, Bowler Schnackenberg Skipper: David Barnes Crew: 32

As soon as Michael Fay's outstanding 12 Metre the *Plastic Fantastic* had been put to bed after the 1987 event, he decided to lay Dennis Conner and his winning San Diego syndicate an interesting wager (Fay's experience of horse racing was still far greater than that of yacht racing).

Fay had been deeply wounded by Conner's onslaught on the validity of his fibre-glass boat, the first such yacht to race for the America's Cup, and had been harbouring a plot which would, he hoped, also get the Cup back on an even keel. Not averse to reading a little Cup history, Fay was not only aware of the ten-month challenge rule but also that the 'Deed of Gift', although limiting the minimum waterline length for the competing yachts, placed no such restrictions on the maximum length. Indeed, as the race had deteriorated over the years into more of a regatta between a proliferation of outmoded 12 Metres, why not go back half a century and invite Conner and his syndicate to put their money on a duel to be fought with just one 'high tech' superyacht apiece?

Michael Fay's September 1988 challenge was received by the San Diego Yacht Club on 15 July 1987 with astonishment, but they were men 'trained' before the mast, and the idea of building a defender in such a short period of time failed to rattle them. But it must have seemed to Dennis Conner and his team that Fay's challenge was inevitably going to level the odds and possibly deny them the opportunity of a more rewarding defence later on. During the winter Conner, appearing at a dinner in celebration of his 1987 Cup victory, told a hushed audience that the vast yacht Michael Fay was about to unleash, crewed in a way that had not been seen since the successful Cup defence by the mighty *Reliance* in 1903, would be no match for the boat planned by the San Diego Yacht Club, which would be sailed by a mere handful of men.

It was inevitable that such America's Cup bravado would soon take both parties to the court room, for Michael Fay was determined to see the now unveiled, and in his opinion illegal, catamaran off the water. But the New York Supreme Court judge Carmen Ciparick ruled that the verdict should be deferred until after the match, which was to be decided by the best of three races starting on 7 September. As expected, the catamaran won by a substantial margin in the first two races, but for Dennis Conner it must have seemed a hollow victory. Back in the courts again the Cup was, for a moment, awarded to the ecstatic New Zealanders – but only to be returned, on appeal, to the team from San Diego. For most enthusiasts the spirit of the America's Cup appeared to be finally in ashes.

The catamaran *Stars & Stripes* defeating *New Zealand*

Stars & Stripes *New Zealand*

1992
AMERICA³ defeats
IL MORO DI VENEZIA

America³
San Diego
Yacht Club
(4 boats)

Syndicate: America
Syndicate Head: Bill Koch
Designers:
Peterson, Meldner, Milgram,
Pugh, Reichel, Moeyersom
Builders: Hercules Aerospace, Goetz
Helmsmen: Buddy Melges, Bill Koch

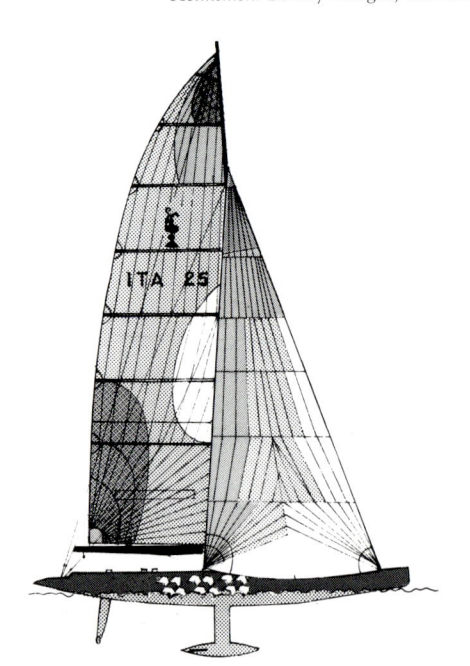

Il Moro di Venezia
Compagnia
della Vela
(5 boats)

Syndicate: Compagnia della Vela
Chairman: Raul Gardini
Designers:
German Frers, Hopkins, Sena
Builders: Tencara (Montedison)
Helmsman: Paul Cayard

While the contentious 1988 challenge was taking place, Bruce Farr, designer of *New Zealand*, was one of those to realise that without a determined initiative, the reputation of the America's Cup was on the line. He therefore helped convene a meeting of the world's leading yacht designers to thrash out the specifications of a new 'controversy-free' class which would take the race well into the next century.

It was generally agreed that the new America's Cup yacht should be more spectacular and testing for the crews than the ageing 12 Metres class, but some potential challengers, fearing a considerable escalation in building costs, argued that it would be possible to fit the existing 12s, or 'Super 12s' as they would be called, with larger rigs by adding as much as 10ft (3m) to the height of their masts. Building these yachts, they calculated, would cost just US$750,000 compared with $1,500,000 for the alternative suggestion of an entirely new class of 75-footers.

Before World War II America's Cup yachts had always been larger and costlier than any other racing class, and now, once again, the dignity of the competition seemed to be at stake. With little ceremony the 75-footers won the day and by the end of March 1990 the first of this new International Class had been unveiled in France. Named simply *F1*, she immediately became the focus of attention, and Marc Pajot, her skipper, was quick to point out that 'sailing this boat is totally different. She is faster, more sensitive and more demanding for the crew, who must handle a huge sail area.'

With the advent of the new Class came a flurry of revised rules and regulations, such as on-the-water umpiring instead of protest by jury, and a remodelled course to give the race better spectator appeal. Yachts were now to be fitted with two compulsory robot cameras, with challengers and defenders splitting the television revenue. But just as the great competitor Sir Thomas Lipton, one-time master of advertising, could not have envisaged the vast media coverage that the America's Cup now enjoys, competing syndicates could not have foreseen the growing world economic slump, which by early 1991 made such potential earnings seem all the more appealing. Even Dennis Conner, hoping to raise some US$20 million, discovered that corporate sponsorship was becoming hard to nail down.

Of the fifteen challengers with boats in the water a year before the 1992 match only ten remained in contention at the start of the elimination series. Once the new IACC breed of yachts was launched the costs, influenced by the big spenders, had quickly escalated to approximately US$4 million for each boat, which included a $750,000 carbon-fibre mast.

Two entries had been received, surprisingly, from Russia, at that time in a state of domestic turmoil. A bitter struggle followed between them, one challenge ending with an unfinished yacht in San Diego harbour and the other with no yacht at all, after a truck transporting her equipment from St Petersburg to the port of Tallinn was hijacked.

The situation was not much better back at the ranch. The America's Cup Organising Committee was in a financial mess, having seemingly failed to appreciate the immense cost of running the event. The unfortunate defence, mainly conducted in the courtroom, of the 1988 raid by New Zealand, had drained their coffers dry, and the situation had been made worse by the reduction in the number of challengers from the 23 originally estimated. Those remaining now decided to help out by lending the ACOC US$1 million to finalize the vital broadcasting arrangements.

But somehow San Diego felt, with its sprawling city and massive Naval dockyard, just too impersonal for the cream of world yachties, and on the other side of the harbour wall the port commissioner was heard to say 'The Cup has no appeal for the community here. It is not the Super Bowl.' Some would have preferred, as Dennis Conner had once suggested, for the Cup to have been contested in the more demanding conditions he had experienced while training off Hawaii.

The 1992 America's Cup was dominated, as is the nature of the beast, by money. Where the organising committee lacked it on shore, two syndicates, one challenger and one defender, had more than enough lucre to rule the Californian waves. Italy's *Il Moro di Venezia* syndicate, headed by Italian industrialist Raul Gardini, kicked off by building their own boatyard, and with the small change, kindly provided by the Ferruzzi-Montedison empire, they constructed five state of the art yachts. Bill Koch, a billionaire amateur yachtsman with a penchant for riding rapids in a canoe, quickly matched the Italians by hiring a team of 200 technicians and then spending some $70m on four hulls, seven masts, nine keels and hundreds of sails. The main protagonists had locked horns.

Sir Michael Fay, not to be outdone, had meanwhile established a highly efficient development programme away from the crowd on the southwestern perimeter of San Diego harbour. Often the first to spring surprises, Bruce Farr's innovative bowsprit fitted to *New Zealand* soon had them winning the challengers' Louis Vuitton Cup by 13-1. Paul Cayard, skipper of *Il Moro*, objected, and after months of deliberation the race jury decided that although bowsprits were permitted, using them as an outrigger was not. Fifty thousand New Zealanders were expected in San Diego for the final round of the challengers' series, but they were to be disappointed when their yacht never regained the initiative. Meanwhile the immaculate French entry *Ville de Paris* and the Japanese, Swedish, Spanish and two Australian syndicates left for home.

The final could almost have been between two sailmakers. Team Dennis Conner had already conceded defeat to the overwhelming fire power of Bill Koch's arsenal, when *America³* came out flying such a silvery white sail that the crew all had to wear sunglasses. Claiming that his new fibre was '50 per cent lighter and twice as strong as Kevlar', Koch, sometimes taking the helm from sixty-two-year-old Buddy Melges, moved into top gear mindful that Gardini had spent a fortune developing an ultra light, hugely expensive sailcloth woven with black carbon thread that *Il Moro*'s skipper had described as 'the biggest innovation in sailmaking for ten years.' For a breathless moment Cayard squared the series, but at 3-1 down Gardini admitted, 'We are waiting for death'. It was not long to follow.

The racing was close. Through four months of trials and the Cup itself, Il Moro di Venezia scored 27 wins, losing 16 and the defender America³ scored 28 wins, losing 10 races

Bill Koch, the owner, often helmed the boat himself

America³   *Il Moro di Venezia*

1995
BLACK MAGIC defeats YOUNG AMERICA

Black Magic
Royal
New Zealand
Yacht Squadron

Syndicate: Team New Zealand
Syndicate Head: Peter Blake
Designers: Peterson, Davidson, Alan Williams, Schnackenberg (co-ord)
Builders: McMullen & Wing
Helmsman: Russell Coutts

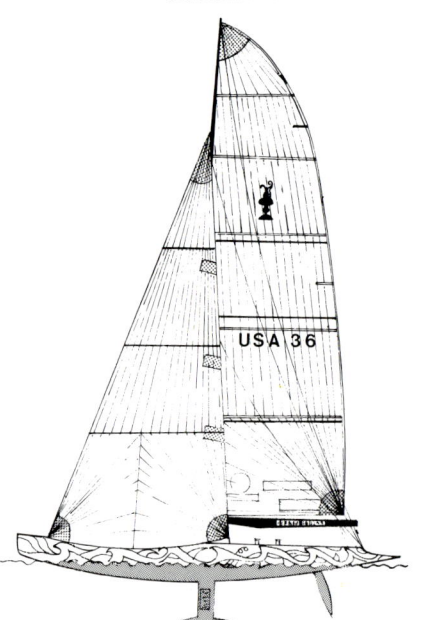

Young America
San Diego
Yacht Club
(One of 3 boats from different syndicates)

Syndicate: Team Dennis Conner
Syndicate Head: Dennis Conner
Designers: Bruce Nelson and team
Builders: Goetz
Helmsmen:
Paul Cayard, Dennis Conner

After his winning 1992 campaign Bill Koch had openly admitted that one of his support boats, *Guzzini*, had fired low-level lasers at the other competitors in order to calculate their performances. The old days of watching for bubbles in the dock were obviously past and spying had gone too far, so in 1995 syndicates unanimously agreed to allow their yachts to drop their skirts and to blatantly flash their bottoms.

That was not all that the yachts were to show off, for thanks to the previous rule change which allowed syndicates to advertise during racing, by 1995 hulls had become so tattooed with graffiti that yachting purists shuddered. But those who had objected to the change from 12 Metres to International America's Cup Class boats had already had to eat humble pie. Bill Koch, who in 1992 had spent some $70m to secure 134 ounces of silver mug, had never gained much of a race advantage and his margin of victory in the final reckoning against the Italian challenger averaged just 50.6 seconds, making it, as had been 'planned' for the new class of boats, the closest America's Cup final of all time!

The reason that this 'planning' now went wrong was entirely due to two black torpedoes fired, late in 1994, at the guts of the American Defenders from the direction of New Zealand.

The success of New Zealand's opening salvo was due to the IACC rule which allowed designers to experiment, without a rating penalty, on reducing beam below an upper limit of 18ft (5.5m). Doug Peterson, who had played a large part in the design of Bill Koch's slimline 1992 winner *America³*, had had a lifetime's experience of the capricious winds and often confused waters off San Diego, and he knew that, unlike the fuller body of *Stars and Stripes* favoured by the old campaigner Dennis Conner and later to be butchered without mercy, a narrower hull with a lower drag ratio held considerable advantages. In this he demonstrated that computers, although more than capable of simplifying the designer's work, were not so hot at reading the complex forces generated by such fickle winds and weather. Surprisingly, no other designer moved as far as Peterson in the same direction.

One of seven challengers from five nations, 'Team New Zealand' had set out to prove that money was not everything. Operating on a conservative budget (in America's Cup terms) of just US$15m, it soon became apparent, as they started carving up the opposition, that it was not just the speed of their yachts that gave them an advantage, but also years of match racing experience and determined preparation. Sir Michael Fay, the New Zealander behind the country's three previous attempts, put it nicely: 'They didn't get the yacht off the shelf, you know; it was a fine team effort.' Needless to say, he made no mention of his own valiant efforts that had laid the keel.

A second 'Win New Zealand' team had entered a yacht NZL-39 designed by Bruce Farr and sailed by Chris Dickson. Together with the Spanish *Rioja de Espana*, the two Japanese *Nippons*, the French *France 2 & 3*, again skippered by Marc Pajot, and two Australian syndicates fielding *oneAustralia* and *Sydney 95*, it had all the ingredients of an exciting elimination series. But so dominant were 'Team New Zealand' with their chosen yacht *Black Magic* (in 1870 the schooner *Magic* won the first America's Cup to be held in the USA) that the 1995 Louis Vuitton Cup will otherwise be remembered only for a shipwreck!

OneAustralia had, it seemed, been built, much as the Cup winner *Reliance* had been built in 1903, to extreme specifications. The 20-knot conditions on that March day had been too much for her and John Bertrand, who had skippered *Australia II* when she won the epic Cup battle of 1983, could only watch, accompanied by the rest of the world on television, as his yacht sank vertically below the briny, like a stone.

The defender trials were memorable for quite a different reason – the first ever women's crew to take part in the America's Cup. Nearly 1,000 American ladies had applied to Bill Koch for the job, ranging from sailors to weightlifters; but was it any more than a media stunt unworthy of such a noble competition? In early April a sudden-death sail-off between Koch's second boat *Mighty Mary* and *Stars and Stripes* was well won by the women's team, plus one male 'tactician', not knowing that a deal was being hammered out on shore to keep the wily Dennis Conner, plagued by a slower boat, in the defenders' finals. 'We felt out of the loop,' stated a lady crew member. Perhaps they were never in it.

On May 1, in an attempt to fend off the threatening New Zealanders with the strongest possible war machine, Conner, who had narrowly won the final race, made an unprecedented move: substitutions being denied to challengers, he chartered *Young America*, of the three defending finalists the yacht most likely to succeed. Five days later, with no time to learn her tricks, he was to receive his first trouncing.

The second race was even more disastrous, *Black Magic* winning by over four minutes – the greatest margin since James Ashbury's *Lavonia* was beaten by the defender *Colombia* in 1871.

While Conner and his helmsman Paul Cayard prepared to walk the plank, Peter Blake, the doyen of New Zealand yachting and the man behind the 1995 challenge, donned his lucky red socks. This led to over 300,000 pairs being sold to his ecstatic countrymen, and half the proceeds went straight to their dock in San Diego. Then, as a giant pair were hoisted on the government building in Wellington, a horse named 'America's Cup' ran at Ellerslie, Auckland, wearing red socks – the last chance, perhaps, for the Americans to lay off their bets!

On May 15 *Black Magic* crossed the line for her fifth consecutive victory to take the America's Cup by storm and thus become only the second boat to grab it from the might of the United States in the Cup's 144-year history. In five months on the water she had lost just one race.

Black Magic led round all 30 marks in her 5:0 defeat of Young America. Over 43 races sailed during the competition the super-yacht won by an average margin of 3min 6sec

By 1995 hulls had become tattooed with graffitti

Black Magic   Young America

2000
BLACK MAGIC defeats LUNA ROSSA

Black Magic
Royal
New Zealand
Yacht Squadron

Syndicate: Team New Zealand
Syndicate Head: Sir Peter Blake KBE
Designers: Laurie Davidson & Clay Oliver
Helmsmen: Russell Coutts, Dean Barker (final race)

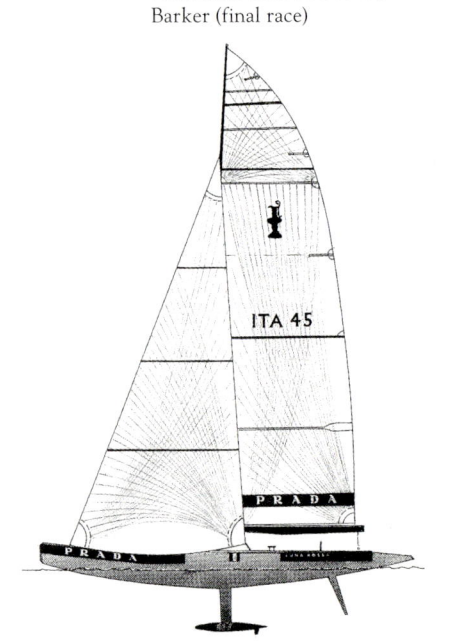

Luna Rossa
YC
Punta Ala

Syndicate: Prada America's Cup Challenge 2000
Syndicate Head: Patrizio Bertelli
Designers: Doug Paterson, German Frers brothers & David Egan
Helmsman: Francesco de Angelis

Had the millennium gone to their heads and the America's Cup yacht designers gone barmy? As the Louis Vuitton elimination races got under sail in Auckland on 18 October 1999, it seemed that several of the sleek new arrivals were not built for the exacting conditions of the Hauraki Gulf and were no stronger than a Louis Vuitton suitcase!

Designing high-performance hulls was becoming more difficult, but was it the designers who were at fault? *Young America* (*USA-53*), the pride of the cash-strapped New York Yacht Club, was the first to go. She had just completed a tack in an early November duel when she buckled like a bent banana in less than 20 knots of wind. Although the rules allowed for shifting weight, surely her diet had been checked a thousand times! But Bruce Farr, her designer, was unwilling to accept any criticism. The failure 'was not a result of a fault in the engineering', he stated, 'or of design.'

Stars and Stripes, Dennis Conner's only child, was the next to fall apart. In just 16 knots of wind the running backstays lifted the bulkhead clean out of the hull, ripping up the cockpit floor. At the same time, she almost lost her mast, a fate which had already struck the Japanese yacht *Asura* with disastrous consequences – plus a hefty $300,000 bill.

One wise old salt had commented that the America's Cup 2000 would be won less by the boat and more by the crew. Certainly the troubled waters of the Gulf were already highlighting more human than design errors. The America's Cup yachts now had such fine tolerances that they had to be handled like eggs! Nippon had already accepted that their dismasting was due to a winch being released too early, and *Young America*'s skipper, Ed Baird, was the first to agree that his boat had folded when he tacked across a couple of steep waves with 'the wrong kind of span'. 'Dirty Dennis', now sporting a cleaner image, was not so forthcoming. 'The sea,' he said, 'was quite calm at the time and my guys do not make such mistakes.'

Crew preparation had not been the best. Only Prada, the Italian's two-boat, US$70 million entry, had escaped criticism, having spent more time on the water than many of the other teams combined. The year before the 150th anniversary of the Cup, it seemed that the lesson would never sink in. Time and again, boats are launched at the eleventh hour without a 'cat's in hell' chance of winning. Such a fate awaited *Spirit of Britain*, still being tank-tested in the summer of 1998. When her challenge was abandoned a year later, even her most ardent supporters breathed a sigh of relief.

While Britain was booming, financial pressures in Japan had cut the Nippon challenge to the bone. Yet Peter Gilmour, her skipper, and her inexperienced crew were to perform well, as was the Spanish entry, also entering for a third time under the skilful hand of Pedro Campos. Of the eleven challengers, including Australian Syd Fischer's final effort, only John Kolius's *Abracadabra* failed to take advantage of the new 3DL moulded sails, while the Swiss Fast 2000 boat's double keels were a technical flop. *America True*, Dawn Riley's entry from San Francisco, sailed slower with every innovation, but not so her compatriot *AmericaOne*, driven unerringly to the Louis Vuitton finals by Paul Cayard, who was accused of giving away his bonus race to *Stars and Stripes*. But despite their late run, team Dennis Conner failed to capitalise on this gift from 'god' and the greatest competitor of them all was caught wiping his eyes. Team Prada's *Luna Rossa*, who richly deserved their place in the finals, would have suffered the same fate, but her skipper, Francesco de Angelis, was saved by the bell when France's *Le Defi* lost her trim tab while performing miracles.

In mid January two new black rocket ships lifted up their skirts. 'These yachts are built tough,' joked Sir Peter Blake, revelling in the fact that *AmericaOne* was still suffering equipment failure and the Cup itself had no restrictions on wind velocity. But it was Team Prada that won the Louis Vuitton 5-4 to challenge Team New Zealand – the first time in 149 years of America's Cup history that the USA was not represented.

Those who had flocked to Auckland to see a dramatic finish, however, were to be sadly disappointed, not least by the surprising lack of wind. The opening race due to be held on 19 February, had to be postponed for two days. When it was finally held, a vast crowd watched Team New Zealand's *Black Magic* (NZL 60) cruise home in a shallow breeze, conditions that were thought to favour the sleek platinum-painted *Luna Rossa*. Race two was also disastrous for the Italians, when a crew member was gashed on the head while removing debris from the keel. Race three went again to the Kiwis, who never failed to grab the best side of the course, as did race four, won by Russell Coutts on his birthday by over one-and-a-half minutes. The boats seemed reasonably well matched, but it was the ruthless efficiency of the *Black Magic* crew, helped by a wind spotter high up the mast, that made the black boat seem invincible.

The final showdown of the 30th America's Cup ended in a clean sweep, this time with Dean Barker, the former world youth champion, proudly taking the Kiwi helm. As the whole of New Zealand once again jumped for joy, a black aircraft banner said it all: 'You Beauty!'

Black Magic takes the America's Cup 5–0 for the second time.

Black Magic *Luna Rossa*

2003
ALINGHI defeats NZL 82

Alinghi
Société Nautique
de Genève

Syndicate: Alinghi Swiss Challenge
Syndicate Head: Ernesto Bertarelli
Skipper: Russell Coutts
Helmsman: Russell Coutts
Tactician: Brad Butterworth
Designers: Rolf Vrolikj, Grant Simmer and Alinghi research and design team
Builder: Decision SA
Sails: North Sails

NZL 82
Royal New
Zealand Yacht
Squadron

Syndicate: Team New Zealand
Syndicate Head: Tom Schnackenberg
Skipper: Dean Barker
Helmsman: Dean Barker
Tactician: Team New Zealand Afterguard
Designers: Tom Schnackenberg, Mike Drummond and Team New Zealand Design Group
Builders: Cookson Boats, Team New Zealand
Sails: North Sails, Team New Zealand

Such was the black boat's victory in 2000 that not in the New Zealand team's wildest dreams would it seem possible for a cloud to obscure the horizon. Yet within a few months of those heady moments in Auckland, like *Black Magic*, the azure blue sky of the southern ocean was to change to the inky hue of a hurricane.

First was the defection by Russell Coutts, Team New Zealand's outstanding helmsman, soon to be followed by no less than two-thirds of their sailors, designers and technicians to clubs from other nations. Second, soon after the magnificent America's Cup Regatta held at Cowes, Isle of Wight, in the summer of 2001, was the shocking murder of Sir Peter Blake by pirates in the mouth of the Amazon River. Sir Peter, a passionate New Zealander who later lived in England, led Team New Zealand's successful America's Cup campaigns in 1995 and 2000, and was the power behind their victories. His famous red socks became the password for success and were worn by a vast army of Team New Zealand supporters at the time of each America's Cup. Later he was to be remembered as the world's greatest sailor.

*Ship, my ship! I seek the West,
And fields and mountains ever blest
Farewell to Middle Earth at last
I see the star above my mast*
J R R Tolkien

READ BY SIR PETER BLAKE'S DAUGHTER
AT HIS MEMORIAL SERVICE

Loyalty, it seems, is no longer a word associated with the America's Cup and by the time the challengers, including three from America, two from Italy, and others from Switzerland, Sweden, France and Great Britain, were gathering in the Hauraki Gulf again for the Louis Vuitton Trophy, many Kiwis, lamenting the loss of their comrades, were boiling over. This anger manifested itself in the BlackHeart campaign, designed to shame those teams, particularly the Alinghi Swiss Challenge and the OneWorld syndicate from Seattle, who had benefited most from the defecting New Zealanders. Some pay packets had become so astronomical by 2002 that they were hard to turn down. As with international football, who could blame sailors who looked for the maximum reward from their super-rich sponsors? Alternatively, traditionalists would argue that in the great days of Sopwith, Lipton and Vanderbilt, such turncoats could expect no less than a keel hauling. But later, when some of the so-called 'traitors' were threatened with grievous bodily harm, the BlackHeart campaign was wisely closed down.

'The dogs of war' had been unleashed with more ferocity than ever, and confident that Team New Zealand had already suffered a mortal blow, the challengers, some with New Zealand helmsmen, closed in for the kill. At first the 'quarry' remained silent. But as one by one the Italian's *Mascalzone Latino*, French entry *Le Defi*, the Swedish boat *Victory*, USA team Dennis Conner's *Stars & Stripes*, the GBR Challenge entry *Wight Lightening* (which fought a great battle after a fifteen-year America's Cup sabbatical), *Prada*, the Italian finalist from 2000, and the American yacht *OneWorld* were all sent back to their kennels, Team New Zealand released the news that they had added to the length of their boat, and thus to its speed, with a revolutionary wrap around 'second skin'. Well done Tom Schnackenberg, Team New Zealand's renowned guru, the sky was turning blue again!

The Louis Vuitton finalists, Swiss billionaire Ernesto Bertarelli's team, sailing *Alinghi*, and American billionaire Larry Ellison's team, sailing ORACLE BMW, were too busy testing new rigs to bother about their bottoms and the Team New Zealand revelation ran off both like water off a duck's back. How could such an appendage be attached within the rules, they asked themselves, particularly under the stress of racing in high winds and rough seas? The gauntlet had been thrown down again with gusto, but 'billionaire belief', as far as *Alinghi* and ORACLE BMW were concerned (both sponsored by men then ranked the 31st and 5th richest in the world), was enough to lift the Cup off the cocky New Zealanders once and for all. Ultimately, after a great struggle, *Alinghi* vanquished ORACLE BMW to do the honours in the finals.

The truth was that the International America's Cup Class (IACC) yachts were again showing themselves as superb match-racing machines but with little room for compromise. Indeed so similar were the lines of the contesting yachts for 2003, that, apart from the importance of signing experienced crews and fitting efficient rigs, just a slight edge on hull design, such as Team New Zealand's 'second skin' or 'Hula' as it became known, could with luck be turned to massive advantage. Peter Harrison was almost as innovative with *Wight Magic*, GBR's reserve boat, but her radical double keel configuration allowed for no third appendage, namely a rudder, and her helmsmen were given insufficient time to get her sailing in the right direction. Preparation for the America's Cup means everything, particularly if you only have Lake Geneva to trial on. Russell Coutts, skipper of *Black Magic* when she won in 2000, now considered by some of his compatriots as their most culpable 'traitor' for deserting to Switzerland, thought more positively. If the skipper's upbringing no longer mattered, neither did the yacht's. *Alinghi*, entered by Société Nautique de Genève, was to be born out of wedlock to the mountains as soon as the 2000 match was completed and bred for the open sea. Should Switzerland win the Cup, the next venue could, as far as her crew were concerned, remain a matter for conjecture. But what they failed to note was that after the disastrous 1881 challenge by a Canadian yacht from the Great Lakes, as recorded earlier, all clubs without an ocean regatta course were banned under the rules from ever competing in the race again!

However, America's Cup rules, as illustrated by the 1988 contest, are, it seems, written to be broken. In February 2003 Team New Zealand and the Alinghi Swiss Challenge set out, instead, to rewrite America's Cup history: the Kiwi boat by breaking its slender boom in the first race and its mast in the fourth race and the Swiss boat, after five clear wins, by being the first team for 152 years to return the Cup to Europe. As a flag depicting the 'Auld Mug' atop the Matterhorn fluttered from *Alinghi*'s mast the unusually despondent Team New Zealand somehow found a different meaning for LOYAL — 'Look Our Yacht's A Lemon'!

Alinghi takes the America's Cup 5–0.

NZL 82　　　　　　　　　　　　　　　Alinghi

2007 ALINGHI defeats NZL 92

Alinghi
Société Nautique de Genève

Syndicate: Alinghi Swiss Challenge
Syndicate Head: Ernesto Bertarelli
Skipper: Brad Butterworth
Helmsman: Ed Baird
Tactician: Brad Butterworth
Designers: Rolf Vrolikj and Alinghi Design Team
Builder: Decision SA
Sails: North Sails

NZL 92
Royal New Zealand Yacht Squadron

Syndicate: Emirates Team New Zealand
Syndicate Head: Grant Dalton
Skipper: Dean Barker
Helmsman: Dean Barker
Tactician: Ray Davies
Designers: ETNZ Design Team
Builders: Cookson Boats, ETNZ
Sails: North Sails

The America's Cup, once noted for the power and sheer beauty of its competitors, particularly the 'J's, had for purists been changing for the worse. Any artist attempting to paint America's Cup Class yachts in 2007 was hard put to convey the grace and vigour of yesteryear, particularly when many of their elegant bows, together with the tops of their once soaring Bermudan mainsails, had been snipped off as if with a pair of scissors! Since 2003 the boat designers and sail makers had been doing their worst, creating mean, boxy machines with one aim only, to beat the fickle winds likely to dog the bay of Valencia, by stretching the rules to the limit.

Sadly one rule that has been stretched increasingly is the employment of foreign sailors. For 132 years, until the Australians put a foot in the door, the America's Cup was strictly contested between nations. By 2007, however, the financial temptations of jumping ship had become so great that many traditionalists asked themselves if the Cup was degenerating into nothing better than a club football match. However, not for Russell Coutts (Rogues Gallery, page 21) *Alinghi*'s brilliant Kiwi helmsman, who after exchanging words with Ernesto Bertarelli, her billionaire owner, leapt ashore to look for different challenges.

The departure of Russell Coutts, three times winner of the America's Cup, left *Alinghi* wallowing in the water, with the young pretenders including *Shosholoza* from South Africa, *Desafio Espanol 2007*, *Areva Challenge* from France, the *United Internet* team from Germany, the *China Team* challenge, and *+39* from Sicily, together with the older pretenders *Victory Challenge* from Sweden sponsored by Red Bull, and *Mascalzone Latino-Capitalia* from Italy, rubbing their hands with glee. But not for long. After a winter spent tuning up his ship in Arabia, Ed Baird, one the three contenders for *Alinghi*'s wheel, although not best known for his starting skills, soon began reeling in the opposition in a number of 'fleet races', or Louis Vuitton 'Acts', introduced by Ernesto Bertarelli prior to the elimination series for the Louis Vuitton Cup. These races provided an interesting new look, as did the additional hype and apparent air of respectability which surrounded them. Only when the underfunded +39 lost her one and only competitive mast in a collision with the yacht from Germany, did the Cup's build up revert to its more enduring habits of dog eat dog. Masts, apart from hulls, are one of the few remaining areas still covered by nationality rules and their rivals had no intention, in this case, of relaxing them and coming to the rescue!

As opposed to *Alinghi*, whose team consisted of only one Swiss, her owner, among 130 people from 21 nations with a solid core of Kiwis, the yacht with the most nationals on board was Emirates Team New Zealand, led by their formidable countryman Grant Dalton. However, the English helmsman, Ben Ainslie, excelled himself as understudy to *NZL 92*'s skipper, Dean Barker, before the competition began in earnest. Two other old hands at the game, Patrizio Bertelli's *Luna Rossa* the new name for the Prada Challenge from Yacht Club Italiano, and the only challenge from America, Larry Ellison's *BMW ORACLE* from the Golden Gate Yacht Club, San Francisco, with an estimated budget of £80M, were also notching up brownie points. The early stages of the Louis Vuitton Cup were often delayed by light winds. But by the semi-finals the weather had steadied, bringing the triumphant progress of *BMW ORACLE* to an abrupt halt against an inspired *Luna Rossa*, with Chris Dixon, her fiery skipper, getting a clipped ear. Two wins by the *Desafio Espanol* over the Kiwis had the Spanish celebrating as if they had won the Cup itself, but all to no avail, and the Kiwis sailed on to soundly defeat *Luna Rossa* 5–0 in the Louis Vuitton final.

When the two America's Cup opponents finally entered the Spanish bull ring in mid June, it was obvious that despite the one-design rules, they had two very different boats. Emirates Team New Zealand with their aggressive, slab-sided concept, seemed to be banking on lighter airs, as they had done previously in Auckland when their boat fell apart in heavy weather, while Bertarelli's *SUI-100*, the favourite, had a much fuller shape, with stronger winds in mind. The first race held on a lumpy sea with a 15 knot east wind blowing went to *Alinghi*, but in the second race, due to a lighter breeze and some skilful sailing by Dean Barker, the Kiwis grabbed back the lead before the final weather mark, levelling it at 1–1. That night Bertarelli, realising it was going to be no walkover, raised his glass to his chosen port of Valencia not realising that the following race, when the lead changed several times, was to go again to New Zealand. Ed Baird, annoyed that *Alinghi* had already dropped her guard twice, made no mistakes in race four, squaring the score at 2–2. In the fifth race *NZL 92* was romping down the course with a substantial lead when disaster struck — as it had in 2003. The spinnaker blew out in a 16 knot nor'easter, the replacement sail then tangled with the wreckage and a third spinnaker failed to deploy fast enough. *Alinghi* pounced and although the Kiwis fought back gallantly, the game was over. In the sixth race the lead was once again to change dramatically on the second upwind leg, leaving the 'Swiwis', as some were now calling them, needing only one more race to win. Meanwhile on shore, the fight had attracted an unprecedented 75,000 spectators!

At the moment of truth, although the Swiss matador had to wait for decent weather before drawing his sword, it was to pierce the heart of Emirates Team New Zealand with unswerving accuracy. At the top of leg three, the Kiwis were leading, but by not enough to cut across *Alinghi*, cleverly placed by Brad Butterworth, to the mark. Instead Dean Barker tried to dive behind and incurred a penalty. Then, as they trailed *Alinghi* towards the finish, the breeze dropped, the Kiwis charged ahead like a wounded bull, passed *Alinghi* for a final time, circled to shake off their penalty and crossed the line just one second behind. It was a thrilling end to possibly the closest contest in America's Cup history.

NZL 92 is penalised for not keeping clear of Alinghi (left) as they approach the top mark in race seven of the America's Cup. Alinghi went on to win the race by one second and retain the Cup.

Alinghi

NZL 92

THE NEXT AMERICA'S CUP

Société Nautique de Genève

In 2003, when Ernesto Bertarelli chose Valencia as the next battleground for the America's Cup, few realised what an ambitious and visionary plan he had in mind. Just as Newport, Rhode Island, had once become famous in America's Cup history, the £280 million or more to be spent on the port of Valencia and its new and extensive yachting facilities, was not to be a shot in the dark. Bertarelli was determined to win the Cup again and establish Valencia as one of the foremost yachting centres in the world.

Valencia answered the challenge admirably, while continuing to enhance its 'City of the Arts' with some of the most spectacular modern architecture to be seen anywhere.

With the media much in mind, a canal was designed within the old fishing port so that competing yachts could be cheered from both banks as they left, or returned, from the 'Bull Ring' and a contemporary building, the Veles e Vents, with extensive viewing balconies, was built for official functions and for those prepared to pay for elevated ringside seats – 'Romeo', as the northern of the two racecourses was called (better name Manolete!), being well within range. Leaving much of the old fish market intact, syndicate docks, were then built in a wide arc with a pier in the centre for berthing super-yachts. The docks not only consisted of piers and slipways equipped to the highest standards, but imposing buildings with integral shops where syndicates could sell their own nautical paraphernalia. At the same time a new 700 berth marina, yet to be filled, was built for visiting yachts.

Never had a more commercially aware and costly site been built for the America's Cup and seldom in the history of yachting had such a gamble paid off so handsomely. With the next America's Cup likely to be staged in Valencia again, possibly as soon as 2009, some estimates suggested that from the 2007 event alone, the city will benefit to the tune of a staggering £1.5 billion!